Lecture Notes in Computer Science 12560

More information about this subseries at http://www.springer.com/series/7407

Michael Hanus · Claudio Sacerdoti Coen (Eds.)

Functional and Constraint Logic Programming

28th International Workshop, WFLP 2020
Bologna, Italy, September 7, 2020
Revised Selected Papers

 Springer

Editors
Michael Hanus (iD)
Kiel University
Kiel, Germany

Claudio Sacerdoti Coen (iD)
University of Bologna
Bologna, Italy

ISSN 0302-9743   ISSN 1611-3349   (electronic)
Lecture Notes in Computer Science
ISBN 978-3-030-75332-0   ISBN 978-3-030-75333-7   (eBook)
https://doi.org/10.1007/978-3-030-75333-7

LNCS Sublibrary: SL1 – Theoretical Computer Science and General Issues

This Springer imprint is published by the registered company Springer Nature Switzerland AG
The registered company address is: Gewerbestrasse 11, 6330 Cham, Switzerland

Preface

This volume contains the proceedings of the 28th International Workshop on Functional and (Constraint) Logic Programming (WFLP 2020), held entirely online due to the coronavirus pandemic, but formally located in Bologna, Italy. The workshop was held on September 7, 2020, as part of the Bologna Federated Conference on Programming Languages 2020.

WFLP aims at bringing together researchers, students, and practitioners interested in functional programming, logic programming, and their integration. WFLP has a reputation for being a lively and friendly forum, and it is open for presenting and discussing work in progress, technical contributions, experience reports, experiments, reviews, and system descriptions.

WFLP 2020 put particular stress on the connections between theory and practice. This stress was reflected in the composition of the Program Committee (PC) and, ultimately, in the program of the workshop. The Call for Papers attracted 19 submissions, of which the PC, after careful and thorough discussions, accepted 10 for presentation at the workshop. All the talks motivated interesting and lively scientific discussions. After the workshop, there was a second independent review to publish the best papers in Springer's Lecture Notes in Computer Science. Each paper was reviewed by at least four PC members using a single-blind reviewing process. The PC selected eight papers for publication, those contained in this volume. The accepted papers cover different areas of functional and logic programming, including code generation, verification, and debugging.

Putting together WFLP 2020 was a team effort. First of all, we would like to thank the authors of the submitted papers. Without the PC we would have had no program either, and we are very grateful to the PC members for their hard work. Supporting the PC were a number of additional reviewers, and we would like to acknowledge their contribution. In general, the reviews were very detailed and helpful, and they produced constructive criticism.

A special thanks goes to the Computer Science and Engineering Department of the University of Bologna for hosting online all the events that were part of the Bologna Federated Conference on Programming Languages 2020.

January 2021

Michael Hanus
Claudio Sacerdoti Coen

Organization

Program Committee Chairs

Michael Hanus   University of Kiel, Germany
Claudio Sacerdoti Coen   University of Bologna, Italy

Program Committee

Sergio Antoy   Portland State University, USA
Demis Ballis   University of Udine, Italy
Moreno Falaschi   Università di Siena, Italy
Herbert Kuchen   University of Muenster, Germany
Dale Miller   Inria and École Polytechnique, France
Konstantinos Sagonas   Uppsala University, Sweden
Enrico Tassi   Inria, France
Janis Voigtländer   University of Duisburg-Essen, Germany
Johannes Waldmann   HTWK Leipzig, Germany

Additional Reviewers

Jan C. Dageförde
Andy Jost
Rudy Matela Braquehais
Heinrich Apfelmus

Contents

Programming Paradigms

SOS Rules for Equivalences of Reaction Systems

Linda Brodo[1], Roberto Bruni[2], and Moreno Falaschi[3(✉)]

[1] Dipartimento di Scienze Economiche e Aziendali, Università di Sassari,
Sassari, Italy
[2] Dipartimento di Informatica, Università di Pisa, Pisa, Italy
[3] Dipartimento di Ingegneria dell'Informazione e Scienze Matematiche,
Università di Siena, Siena, Italy
moreno.falaschi@unisi.it

Abstract. Reaction Systems (RSs) are a successful computational framework inspired by biological systems. A RS combines a set of entities with a set of reactions over them. Entities can be provided by an external context, used to enable or inhibit each reaction, and also produced by reactions. RS semantics is defined in terms of an (unlabelled) rewrite system: given the current set of entities, a rewrite step consists of the application of all and only the enabled reactions. In this paper we define, for the first time, a compositional labelled transition system for RSs with recursive and nondeterministic contexts, in the structural operational semantics (SOS) style. This is achieved by distilling a signature whose operators directly correspond to the ingredients of RSs and by defining some simple SOS inference rules for any such operator. The rich information recorded in the labels allows us to define an assertion language to tailor behavioural equivalences on some specific properties or entities. The SOS approach is suited to drive additional enhancements of RSs along features such as quantitative measurements of entities and communication between RSs. The SOS rules have been also exploited to design a prototype implementation in logic programming.

Keywords: SOS rules · Reaction systems · Assertions · Logic programming

1 Introduction

Labelled Transition Systems (LTSs) are a powerful structure to model the behaviour of interacting processes. An LTS can be conveniently defined following the Structural Operational Semantics (SOS) approach [25,27]. Given a signature, an SOS system assigns some inference rules to each operator of the language: the conclusion of each rule is the transition of a composite term, which is determined

Research supported by MIUR PRIN 201784YSZ5 *ASPRA*, by U. of Pisa PRA_2018_66 *DECLWARE*, by U. of Sassari: Fondo di Ateneo per la ricerca 2020.

M. Hanus and C. Sacerdoti Coen (Eds.): WFLP 2020, LNCS 12560, pp. 3–21, 2021.
https://doi.org/10.1007/978-3-030-75333-7_1

by those of its constituents (appearing as premises of the rule). The SOS approach has been particularly successful in the area of process algebras [20, 22, 26].

Reaction Systems (RSs) [8] are a computational framework inspired by systems of living cells. Its constituents are a finite set of entities and a finite set of reactions acting on entities. A reaction is a triple (R, I, P) where R is the set of reactants (entities whose presences is needed to enable the reaction), I is the set of inhibitors (entities whose absence is needed to enable the reaction) and P is the set of products (entities that are produced if the reaction takes place and that will be made available at the next step). After their introduction, RSs have shown to be a quite general computational model whose application ranges from the modelling of biological phenomena [1–3, 14], and molecular chemistry [24] to theoretical foundations of computing. The semantics of RSs is defined as an unlabelled rewrite system whose states are set of entities (coming from an external context or produced at the previous step). Given the current set of entities, a rewrite step consists of the application of all and only the enabled reactions. Given a context sequence, the behaviour of an RS is uniquely determined and the corresponding (unlabelled, deterministic) transition system is finite.

Here we will define, for the first time, an LTS semantics in the SOS style for RSs with enhanced contexts. First we fix a process signature whose operators pinpoint the basic structure of a RS. We have operators for entities and reactions. For contexts we exploit some classic process algebraic operators (action prefix, sum and recursion). This way we can recursively define contexts that possibly exhibit nondeterministic behaviour, as sometimes have already appeared in the literature [9, 21]. Even though we enrich the expressiveness of contexts, the overall LTS still remains finite. The SOS approach has several advantages: 1) compositionality, the behaviour of each composite system is defined in term of the behaviours of its constituents; 2) each transition label conveys all the activities connected to that computational step; 3) the definition of contexts is better integrated in the framework; 4) different context sequences can be studied at once; 5) it is now easier to extend the concept of RSs by adding new operators; 6) SOS rules facilitate implementation in a declarative language and the application of standard techniques for defining equivalences between processes.

The transition labels of our LTS are so rich of information that standard notion of behavioural equivalence (like traces or bisimulation) are too fine grain. For studying RSs, one is often interested in focusing on some entities and disregard others, like exploiting a microscope to enhance certain details and ignore others that fall out of the picture. To this aim, following the ideas in our previous paper [10], we propose an assertion language built over the transition labels, and we make the definition of behavioural and logical equivalences parametric w.r.t. such assertions. This way, it is possible to consider different RSs as equivalent for some purposes or to distinguish them for other purposes. Furthermore, we develop suitable behavioural equivalences for RS processes, and show the correspondence between a coinductive definition in terms of bisimilarity and its logical counterpart *à la* Hennessy-Milner.

We have developed a prototype implementation in logic programming of our semantic framework available online, as we describe in Sect. 5. Our interpreter allows the user to check automatically on the labels for a given RS the validity of formulas expressed in our variant of the Hennessy-Milner logic combined with the assertions specified in our language.

Related Work. The work by Kleijn et al. [21] studies two versions of LTS for RS: one with state-oblivious context controller, and the other with state-aware context controller. In the first version, the labels only record the entities provided by the context, and in the second one the labels also provide the entities composing the actual state. The last choice allows one to decide which entities the context should provide. Differently, we give a process algebra-style definition of the RS, where the SOS rules produce informative transition labels, including context specification, allowing different kinds of analysis.

There are some previous works based on bisimulation applied to models for biological systems. Barbuti et al. [4] define a classical setting for bisimulation for two formalisms: the Calculus of Looping Sequences, which is a rewriting system, and the Brane Calculi, which is based on process calculi. Bisimulation is used to verify properties of the regulation of lactose degradation in Escherichia coli and the EGF signalling pathway. These calculi allow the authors to model membranes' behaviour. Cardelli et al. [12] present two quantitative behavioral equivalences over species of a chemical reaction network with semantics based on ordinary differential equations. Bisimulation identifies a partition where each equivalence class represents the exact sum of the concentrations of the species belonging to that class. Bisimulation also relates species that have identical solutions at all time points when starting from the same initial conditions. Both the mentioned formalisms [4,12] adopt a classical approach to bisimulation.

In Brodo et al. [9,10] we derived similar results to those presented here by encoding RSs into cCNA, a multi-party process algebra (a variant of the link-calculus [5,6]). In comparison with the encoding of RS in cCNA, we get here a much simpler computational model, closer to the syntax of RSs, preserving the expressiveness at the level of transition labels.

Structure of the Paper. Section 2 recalls the basics of RSs. The original contribution starts from Sect. 3, where: 1) we introduce the syntax and SOS rules of a novel process algebra for RSs, 2) we show how to encode RSs as processes, 3) we prove a tight semantic correspondence between RSs and their encodings. Section 4 shows the correspondence between assertion-based coinductive equivalences and their logical counterpart *à la* Hennessy-Milner. A prototype implementation in logic programming of our semantic framework is briefly described in Sect. 5. Further extensions of RSs that build on our theory are sketched in Sect. 6. Some concluding remarks are in Sect. 7.

2   Reaction Systems

The theory of Reaction Systems (RSs) [8] was born in the field of Natural Computing to model the behaviour of biochemical reactions in living cells.

We use the term *entities* to denote generic molecular substances (e.g., atoms, ions, molecules) that may be present in the states of a biochemical system. The main mechanisms that regulate the functioning of a living cell are *facilitation* and *inhibition*. These mechanisms are based on the presence and absence of entities and are reflected in the basic definitions of RSs.

Definition 1 (Reaction). *Let S be a (finite) set of entities. A reaction in S is a triple $a = (R, I, P)$, where $R, I, P \subseteq S$ are finite, non empty sets and $R \cap I = \emptyset$.*

The sets R, I, P are the sets of *reactants*, *inhibitors*, and *products*, respectively. All reactants are needed for the reaction to take place. Any inhibitor blocks the reaction. Products are the outcome of the reaction. Since R and I are not empty, all products are produced from at least one reactant and every reaction can be inhibited. We let $rac(S)$ be the set of all reactions in S.

Definition 2 (Reaction System). *A Reaction System (RS) is a pair $\mathcal{A} = (S, A)$ s.t. S is a finite set, and $A \subseteq rac(S)$ is a finite set of reactions in S.*

The theory of RSs is based on three assumptions: **no permanency**, any entity vanishes unless it is sustained by a reaction. In fact, a living cell would die for lack of energy, without chemical reactions; **no counting**, the basic model of RSs is very abstract and qualitative, i.e. the quantity of entities that are present in a cell is not taken into account; **threshold nature of resources**, we assume that either an entity is available for all reactions, or it is not available at all.

Definition 3 (Reaction Result). *Given a (finite) set of entities S, and a subset $W \subseteq S$, we define the following:*

1. *Let $a = (R, I, P) \in rac(S)$ be a reaction in S. The result of a on W, denoted by $res_a(W)$, is defined by:*

$$res_a(W) \triangleq \begin{cases} P & \text{if } en_a(W) \\ \emptyset & \text{otherwise} \end{cases}$$

where the enabling predicate is defined by $en_a(W) \triangleq R \subseteq W \wedge I \cap W = \emptyset$.
2. *Let $A \subseteq rac(S)$ be a finite set of reactions. The result of A on W, denoted by $res_A(W)$, is defined by: $res_A(W) \triangleq \bigcup_{a \in A} res_a(W)$.*

Living cells are seen as open systems that react with the external environment. The behaviour of a RS is formalized in terms of *interactive processes*.

Definition 4 (Interactive Process). *Let $\mathcal{A} = (S, A)$ be a RS and let $n \geq 0$. An n-steps interactive process in $\mathcal{A}$ is a pair $\pi = (\gamma, \delta)$ s.t. $\gamma = \{C_i\}_{i \in [0,n]}$ is the context sequence and $\delta = \{D_i\}_{i \in [0,n]}$ is the result sequence, where $C_i, D_i \subseteq S$ for any $i \in [0, n]$, $D_0 = \emptyset$, and $D_{i+1} = res_A(D_i \cup C_i)$ for any $i \in [0, n-1]$. We call $\tau = W_0, \ldots, W_n$ with $W_i \triangleq C_i \cup D_i$, for any $i \in [0, n]$ the state sequence.*

The context sequence γ represents the environment. The result sequence δ is entirely determined by γ and A. Each state W_i in τ is the union of two sets: the context C_i at step i and the result set $D_i = res_A(W_{i-1})$ from the previous step.

Given a context sequence γ, we denote by γ^k the shift of γ starting at the k-th step. The shift notation will come in handy to draw a tight correspondence between the classic semantics of RS and the newly proposed SOS specification.

Definition 5 (Sequence shift). *Let $\gamma = \{C_i\}_{i \in [0,n]}$ a context sequence. Given a positive integer $k \leq n$ we let $\gamma^k = \{C_{i+k}\}_{i \in [0,n-k]}$. Note that $\gamma^0 = \gamma$.*

We conclude this section with a simple example of RS.

Example 1. Here we consider a toy RS defined as $\mathcal{A} = (S, A)$ where the set $S = \{a, b, c\}$ only contains three entities, and the set of reactions $A = \{a_1\}$ only contains the reaction $a_1 = (\{a, b\}, \{c\}, \{b\})$, to be written more concisely as (ab, c, b). Then, we consider a $4-steps$ interactive process $\pi = (\gamma, \delta)$, where $\gamma = \{C_0, C_1, C_2, C_3\}$, with $C_0 = \{a, b\}$, $C_1 = \{a\}$, $C_2 = \{c\}$, and $C_3 = \{c\}$; and $\delta = \{D_0, D_1, D_2, D_3\}$, with $D_0 = \emptyset$, $D_1 = \{b\}$, $D_2 = \{b\}$, and $D_3 = \emptyset$. Then, the resulting state sequence is

$$\tau = W_0, W_1, W_2, W_3 = \{a, b\}, \{a, b\}, \{b, c\}, \{c\}.$$

In fact, it is easy to check that, e.g., $W_0 = C_0$, $D_1 = res_A(W_0) = res_A(\{a, b\}) = \{b\}$ because $en_a(W_0)$, and $W_1 = C_1 \cup D_1 = \{a\} \cup \{b\} = \{a, b\}$.

3   SOS Rules for Reaction Systems

Inspired by classic process algebras, such as CCS [22], we introduce a syntax for RSs that resembles their original presentation and then equip each operator with some SOS inference rules that define its behaviour. This way: (1) we establish a strong correspondence between terms of the signature and RSs; (2) we derive an LTS semantics for each RS, where the states are terms, each transition corresponds to a step of the RS and transition labels retain some information needed for compositionality; (3) we pave the way to the RS enhancements in Sect. 6.

Definition 6 (RS processes). *Let S be a set of entities. An RS process P is any term defined by the following grammar:*

$$
\begin{aligned}
&\mathsf{P} ::= [\mathsf{M}] \\
&\mathsf{M} ::= (R, I, P) \mid D \mid K \mid \mathsf{M}|\mathsf{M} \\
&\mathsf{K} ::= \mathbf{0} \mid X \mid C.\mathsf{K} \mid \mathsf{K} + \mathsf{K} \mid \operatorname{rec} X.\,\mathsf{K}
\end{aligned}
$$

where $R, I, P \subseteq S$ are non empty sets of entities (with $R \cap I = \emptyset$), $C, D \subseteq S$ are possibly empty set of entitities, and X is a process variable.

An RS process P embeds a *mixture* process M obtained as the parallel composition of some reactions (R, I, P), some set of currently present entities D (possibly the empty set $\emptyset$), and some *context* process K. We write $\prod_{i \in I} M_i$ for the parallel composition of all M_i with $i \in I$. For example, $\prod_{i \in \{1,2\}} M_i = M_1 \mid M_2$.

A process context K is a possibly nondeterministic and recursive system: the nil context **0** stops the computation; the prefixed context $C.K$ says that the entities in C are immediately available to be consumed by the reactions, and then K is the context offered at the next step; the non deterministic choice $K_1 + K_2$ allows the context to behave either as K_1 or K_2; X is a process variable, and rec X. K is the usual recursive operator of process algebras. We write $\sum_{i \in I} K_i$ for the nondeterministic choice between all K_i with $i \in I$.

We say that P and P' are structurally equivalent, written $P \equiv P'$, when they denote the same term up to the laws of commutative monoids (unit, associativity and commutativity) for parallel composition $\cdot | \cdot$, with $\emptyset$ as the unit, and the laws of idempotent and commutative monoids for choice $\cdot + \cdot$, with **0** as the unit. We also assume $D_1 | D_2 \equiv D_1 \cup D_2$ for any $D_1, D_2 \subseteq S$.

Remark 1. Note that the (mixture) process $\emptyset$ and the (context) process **0** are not the same: as it will become clear from the operational semantics, the process $\emptyset$ has just a trivial transition to itself, while the process **0** has no outgoing transition and is used to stop the computation.

Definition 7 (RSs as RS processes). *Let $\mathcal{A} = (S, A)$ be a RS, and $\pi = (\gamma, \delta)$ an n-step interactive process in $\mathcal{A}$, with $\gamma = \{C_i\}_{i \in [0,n]}$ and $\delta = \{D_i\}_{i \in [0,n]}$. For any step $i \in [0, n]$, the corresponding RS process $[\![\mathcal{A}, \pi]\!]_i$ is defined as follows:*

$$[\![\mathcal{A}, \pi]\!]_i \triangleq \left[\prod_{a \in A} a \mid D_i \mid K_{\gamma^i} \right]$$

where the context process $K_{\gamma^i} \triangleq C_i.C_{i+1}.\cdots.C_n.\mathbf{0}$ is the sequentialization of the entities offered by γ^i. We write $[\![\mathcal{A}, \pi]\!]$ as a shorthand for $[\![\mathcal{A}, \pi]\!]_0$.

Example 2. Here, we give the encoding of the reaction system, $\mathcal{A} = (S, A)$, defined in Example 1. The resulting RS process is as follows:

$$P = [\![\mathcal{A}, \pi]\!] = [\![(\{a, b, c\}, \{(ab, c, b)\}), \pi]\!] = [(ab, c, b) \mid \emptyset \mid K_\gamma] \equiv [(ab, c, b) \mid K_\gamma]$$

where $K_\gamma = \{a, b\}.\{a\}.\{c\}.\{c\}.\mathbf{0}$, written more concisely as $ab.a.c.c.\mathbf{0}$. Note that $D_0 = \emptyset$ is inessential and can be discarded thanks to structural congruence.

In Definition 7 we have not exploited the entire potentialities of the syntax. In particular, the context K_γ is just a finite sequence of action prefixes induced by the set of entities provided by γ at the various steps. Our syntax allows for more general kinds of contexts as shown in the example below. Nondeterministic contexts can be used to collect several experiments, while recursion can be exploited to extract some regularity in the longterm behaviour of a Reaction System. Together they offer any combination of in-breadth/in-depth analysis.

$$\frac{}{D \xrightarrow{\langle D \rhd \emptyset, \emptyset, \emptyset \rangle} \emptyset} \ (Ent) \qquad \frac{}{C.K \xrightarrow{\langle C \rhd \emptyset, \emptyset, \emptyset \rangle} K} \ (Cxt) \qquad \frac{K[^{\mathrm{rec}\ X.\ K}/_X] \xrightarrow{\langle W \rhd R, I, P \rangle} K'}{\mathrm{rec}\ X.\ K \xrightarrow{\langle W \rhd R, I, P \rangle} K'} \ (Rec)$$

$$\frac{K_1 \xrightarrow{\langle W \rhd R, I, P \rangle} K_1'}{K_1 + K_2 \xrightarrow{\langle W \rhd R, I, P \rangle} K_1'} \ (Suml) \qquad \frac{K_2 \xrightarrow{\langle W \rhd R, I, P \rangle} K_2'}{K_1 + K_2 \xrightarrow{\langle W \rhd R, I, P \rangle} K_2'} \ (Sumr)$$

$$\frac{}{(R, I, P) \xrightarrow{\langle \emptyset \rhd R, I, P \rangle} (R, I, P) \mid P} \ (Pro) \qquad \frac{J \subseteq I \quad Q \subseteq R \quad J \cup Q \neq \emptyset}{(R, I, P) \xrightarrow{\langle \emptyset \rhd J, Q, \emptyset \rangle} (R, I, P)} \ (Inh)$$

$$\frac{M_1 \xrightarrow{\langle W_1 \rhd R_1, I_1, P_1 \rangle} M_1' \quad M_2 \xrightarrow{\langle W_2 \rhd R_2, I_2, P_2 \rangle} M_2' \quad (W_1 \cup W_2 \cup R_1 \cup R_2) \cap (I_1 \cup I_2) = \emptyset}{M_1 \mid M_2 \xrightarrow{\langle W_1 \cup W_2 \rhd R_1 \cup R_2, I_1 \cup I_2, P_1 \cup P_2 \rangle} M_1' \mid M_2'} \ (Par)$$

$$\frac{M \xrightarrow{\langle W \rhd R, I, P \rangle} M' \quad R \subseteq W}{[M] \xrightarrow{\langle W \rhd R, I, P \rangle} [M']} \ (Sys)$$

Fig. 1. SOS semantics of the reaction system processes.

Example 3. Let us consider our running example. Suppose we want to enhance the behaviour of the context by defining a process $K' = K_1 + K_2$ that non-deterministically can behave as K_1 or as K_2, where $K_1 = \mathsf{ab.a.c.c.0}$ (as in Example 2), and $K_2 = \mathrm{rec}\ X.\ \mathsf{ab.a.}X$ (which is a recursive behaviour that allows the reaction to be always enabled). Then we simply define $P' \equiv [(\mathsf{ab}, \mathsf{c}, \mathsf{b}) \mid K']$.

Definition 8 (Label). *A label is a tuple* $\langle W \rhd R, I, P \rangle$ *with* $W, R, I, P \subseteq S$.

In a transition label $\langle W \rhd R, I, P \rangle$, we record the set W of entities currently in the system (produced in the previous step or provided by the context), the set R of entities whose presence is assumed (either because they are needed as reactants on an applied reaction or because their presence prevents the application of some reaction); the set I of entities whose absence is assumed (either because they appear as inhibitors for an applied reaction or because their absence prevents the application of some reaction); the set P of products of all the applied reactions.

Definition 9 (Operational semantics). *The operational semantics of processes is defined by the set of SOS inference rules in Fig. 1.*

The process **0** has no transition. The rule (*Ent*) makes available the entities in the (possibly empty) set D, then reduces to $\emptyset$. As a special instance of (*Ent*), $\emptyset \xrightarrow{\langle \emptyset \rhd \emptyset, \emptyset, \emptyset \rangle} \emptyset$. The rule (*Cxt*) says that a prefixed context process $C.K$ makes available the entities in the set C and then reduces to K. The rule (*Rec*) is the classical rule for recursion. Here, $K[^{\mathrm{rec}\ X.\ K}/_X]$ denotes the process obtained by replacing in K every free occurrence of the variable X with its recursive definition rec X. K. For example rec X. a.b.X $\xrightarrow{\langle a \triangleright \emptyset, \emptyset, \emptyset \rangle}$ b.rec X. a.b.X The rules $(Suml)$ and $(Sumr)$ select a move of either the left or the right component, resp., discarding the other process. The rule (Pro), executes the reaction (R, I, P) (its reactants, inhibitors, and products are recorded the label), which remains available at the next step together with P. The rule (Inh) applies when the reaction (R, I, P) should not be executed; it records in the label the possible causes for which the reaction is disabled: possibly some inhibiting entities $(J \subseteq I)$ are present or some reactants $(Q \subseteq R)$ are missing, with $J \cup Q \neq \emptyset$, as at least one cause is needed for explaining why the reaction is not enabled.[1] The rule (Par) puts two processes in parallel by pooling their labels and joining all the set components of the labels; a sanity check is required to guarantee that there is no conflict between reactants and inhibitors of the applied reactions. Finally, the rule (Sys) requires that all the processes of the systems have been considered, and also checks that all the needed reactants are actually available in the system $(R \subseteq W)$. In fact this constraint can only be met on top of all processes. The check that inhibitors are absent $(I \cap W = \emptyset)$ is not necessary, as is guaranteed by the semantics (see Lemma 3).

Example 4. Let us consider the RS process $P_0 \triangleq [(ab, c, b) \mid ab.a.c.c.0]$ from Example 2. The process P_0 has a unique outgoing transition, whose formal derivation is given below:

$$\frac{\dfrac{}{(ab, c, b) \xrightarrow{\langle \emptyset \triangleright ab, c, b \rangle} (ab, c, b) \mid b} (Pro) \quad \dfrac{}{ab.a.c.c.0 \xrightarrow{\langle ab \triangleright \emptyset, \emptyset, \emptyset \rangle} a.c.c.0} (Cxt)}{\dfrac{(ab, c, b) \mid ab.a.c.c.0 \xrightarrow{\langle ab \triangleright ab, c, b \rangle} (ab, c, b) \mid b \mid a.c.c.0}{[(ab, c, b) \mid ab.a.c.c.0] \xrightarrow{\langle ab \triangleright ab, c, b \rangle} [(ab, c, b) \mid b \mid a.c.c.0]} (Sys)} (Par)$$

The target process $P_1 \triangleq [(ab, c, b) \mid b \mid a.c.c.0]$ has also a unique outgoing transition, namely:

$$P_1 = [(ab, c, b) \mid b \mid a.c.c.0] \xrightarrow{\langle ab \triangleright ab, c, b \rangle} [(ab, c, b) \mid b \mid c.c.0] = P_2$$

Instead the process P_2 has three outgoing transitions, each providing a different justification to the fact that the reaction (ab, c, b) is not enabled:

1. $[(ab, c, b) \mid b \mid c.c.0] \xrightarrow{\langle bc \triangleright c, a, \emptyset \rangle} [(ab, c, b) \mid c.0]$, where the label shows that the presence of c and the absence of a inhibit the reaction;
2. $[(ab, c, b) \mid b \mid c.c.0] \xrightarrow{\langle bc \triangleright c, \emptyset, \emptyset \rangle} [(ab, c, b) \mid c.0]$, where it is only observed that the presence of c has played some role in inhibiting the reaction;

---

[1] Conceptually, one could extend labels to record J and Q in separate positions from R and I, respectively, like in $\langle W \triangleright R, J, I, Q, P \rangle$. However, one would then need to rewrite the side conditions of all the rules by replacing R with $R \cup J$ and I with $I \cup Q$, because the distinction is never exploited in the SOS rules.

3. $[(ab, c, b) \mid b \mid c.c.0] \xrightarrow{\langle bc \triangleright \emptyset, a, \emptyset \rangle} [(ab, c, b) \mid c.0]$, where it is only observed that the absence of a has played some role in inhibiting the reaction.

Notably, the three transitions have the same target process $P_3 \triangleq [(ab, c, b) \mid c.0]$.

Finally, the process P_3 has seven transitions all leading to $P_4 \triangleq [(ab, c, b) \mid 0]$. Their labels are of the form $\langle c \triangleright J, Q, \emptyset \rangle$ with $J \subseteq c$, $Q \subseteq ab$ and $J \cup Q \neq \emptyset$. Each label provides a different explanation why the reaction is not enabled.

The following technical lemmas express some relevant properties of the transition system and are proved by rule induction.

Lemma 1. *If* $M \xrightarrow{\langle W \triangleright R, I, P \rangle} M'$ *then* $M' \equiv M'' \mid P$ *for some* M''.

Lemma 2. *If* $\prod_{a \in A} a \xrightarrow{\langle W \triangleright R, I, P \rangle} M$ *then* $W = \emptyset$ *and* $M \equiv \prod_{a \in A} a \mid P$.

Lemma 3. *If* $M \xrightarrow{\langle W \triangleright R, I, P \rangle} M'$ *then* $(W \cup R) \cap I = \emptyset$.

Lemma 4. *If* $P \xrightarrow{\langle W \triangleright R, I, P \rangle} P'$ *then* $R \subseteq W$ *and* $W \cap I = \emptyset$.

The main theorem shows that the rewrite steps of a RS exactly match the transitions of its corresponding RS process.

Theorem 1. *Let* $\mathcal{A} = (S, A)$ *be a RS, and* $\pi = (\gamma, \delta)$ *an n-step interactive process in* $\mathcal{A}$ *with* $\gamma = \{C_i\}_{i \in [0,n]}$, $\delta = \{D_i\}_{i \in [0,n]}$, *and let* $W_i \triangleq C_i \cup D_i$ *and* $P_i \triangleq [\![\mathcal{A}, \pi]\!]_i$ *for any* $i \in [0, n]$. *Then:*

1. $\forall i \in [0, n-1]$, $P_i \xrightarrow{\langle W \triangleright R, I, P \rangle} P$ *implies* $W = W_i$, $P = D_{i+1}$ *and* $P \equiv P_{i+1}$;
2. $\forall i \in [0, n-1]$, *there exists* $R, I \subseteq S$ *such that* $P_i \xrightarrow{\langle W_i \triangleright R, I, D_{i+1} \rangle} P_{i+1}$.

Remark 2. Note that the process $P_n = [\![\mathcal{A}, \pi]\!]_n = [\prod_{a \in A} a \mid D_n \mid C_n.0]$ has one more transition available (the $(n+1)$-th step from P_0), even if the standard theory of RSs stops the computation after n steps. We thus have additional steps

$$P_n \xrightarrow{\langle W_n \triangleright R_n, I_n, res_A(W_n) \rangle} \left[\prod_{a \in A} a \mid res_A(W_n) \mid 0 \right]$$

for suitable $R_n, I_n \subseteq S$. The target process contains 0 and therefore is deadlock.

Example 4 shows that we can have redundant transitions because of rule (*Inh*). However, they can be easily detected and eliminated by considering a notion of dominance. To this aim we introduce an order relation $\sqsubseteq$ over pairs of set of entities defined as follows:

$$(R', I') \sqsubseteq (R, I) \quad \text{if} \quad R' \subseteq R \wedge I' \subseteq I.$$

Definition 10 (Dominance). *A transition* $P \xrightarrow{\langle W \triangleright R', I', P \rangle} P'$ *is dominated if there exists another transition* $P \xrightarrow{\langle W \triangleright R, I, P \rangle} P'$ *such that* $(R', I') \sqsubset (R, I)$.

Note that in the definition of dominance we require the dominated transition to have the same source and target processes as the dominant transition, and that their labels carry also the same sets W and P.

Finally, we can immediately derive an LTS, whose transitions are written using double arrows, where only dominant transitions are considered. The LTS is defined by the additional SOS rule (Dom) below:

$$\frac{P \xrightarrow{\langle W \triangleright R,I,P \rangle} P' \quad (R,I) = \max_{\sqsubseteq}\{(R',I') \mid P \xrightarrow{\langle W \triangleright R',I',P \rangle} P'\}}{P \xRightarrow{\langle W \triangleright R,I,P \rangle} P'} \ (Dom)$$

In other words, a transition $P \xRightarrow{\langle W \triangleright R,I,P \rangle} P'$ guarantees that any instance of the rule (Inh) is applied in a way that maximizes the sets J and Q (given the overall available entities W).

Example 5. Looking back at Example 4, both transitions $P_2 \xrightarrow{\langle bc \triangleright c,\emptyset,\emptyset \rangle} P_3$ and $P_2 \xrightarrow{\langle bc \triangleright \emptyset,a,\emptyset \rangle} P_3$ are dominated by $P_2 \xrightarrow{\langle bc \triangleright c,a,\emptyset \rangle} P_3$. Therefore, the process $P_2 = [(ab, c, b) \mid b \mid c.c.0]$ has a unique (double-arrow) transition $P_2 \xRightarrow{\langle bc \triangleright c,a,\emptyset \rangle} P_3$.

4   Bio-Simulation

Bisimulation equivalences [28] play a central role in process algebras. They can be defined in terms of coinductive games, of fixpoint theory and of logics. The bisimulation game is played by an attacker and a defender: the former wants to disprove the equivalence between two processes p and q, the latter that p and q are equivalent. The game is turn based: at each turn the attacker picks one process, e.g., p, and one transition $p \xrightarrow{\lambda} p'$ and the defender must reply by picking one transition $q \xrightarrow{\lambda} q'$ of the other process with exactly the same label λ; then the game continues challenging the equivalence between p' and q'. The game ends when the attacker has no transition available, and the defender wins, or when defender cannot match the move of the attacker, and the attacker wins. The defender also wins if the game doesn't end. Then p and q are not equivalent iff the attacker has a winning strategy. There are many variants of the bisimulation for process algebras, for example the barbed bisimulation [23] only considers the execution of invisible actions, and then equates two processes when they expose the same prefixes; for the mobile ambients [11], a process algebra equipped with a reduction semantics, a notion of behavioural equivalence equates two processes when they expose the same ambients [18].

In the case of biological systems, the classical notion of bisimulation can be too concrete. In fact, in a biological soup, a high number of interactions occur every time instant, and generally, biologists are only interested to analyse a small subset of them and to focus on a subset of entities. In the case of RS processes, the labels that we used for the LTS consider too many details and convey too much information: they record the entire information about all the reactions that have been applied in one transition, the entities that acted as reactants, as inhibitors or as products, or that were available in the state. All this information stored in the label is necessary to compose a transition in a modular way. Depending on the application, only a suitable abstraction over the label can be of interest. For this reason, following the approach introduced in Brodo et al. [10], we propose an alternative notion of bisimulation, called *bio-simulation*, that compares two biological systems by restricting the observation to only a limited set of events that are of particular interest. With respect to the work in Brodo et al. [10], here the labels are easier to manage and simpler to parse.

In a way, at each step of the bisimulation game, we want to query our labels about some partial information. To this goal, we define an assertion language to express detailed and partial queries about what happened in a single transition.

Example 6. For instance we would like to express properties about each step of the bio-simulation of a system like the ones below:

1. Has the presence of the entity a been exploited by some reaction?
2. Have the entities a and b been produced by some reaction?
3. Have the entities a or c been provided by the state?
4. Has the reaction (ab, c, b) been applied or not?

As detailed before, in the following we assume that the context can be non-deterministic, otherwise it makes little sense to rely on bisimulation to observe the branching structure of system dynamics.

The bio-simulation approach works as follows: first we introduce an assertion language to abstract away some information from the labels; then we define a bisimilarity equivalence that is parametric to a given assertion, called bio-similarity; finally we give a logical characterisation of bio-similarity, called biological equivalence, by tailoring the classical HML to the given assertion.

4.1   Assertion Language

An assertion is a formula that predicates on the labels of our LTS. The assertion language that we propose is very basic, but can be extended if necessary.

Definition 11 (Assertion Language). *Given a set of entities S, assertions F on S are built from the following syntax, where $E \subseteq S$ and $Pos \in \{W, R, I, P\}$:*

$$F ::= E \subseteq Pos \mid ? \in Pos \mid F \vee F \mid F \wedge F \mid F \char`^ F \mid \neg F$$

Roughly, *Pos* distinguishes different positions in the labels: W stands for entities provided by current state, R stands for reactants, I stands for inhibitors, and P stands for products. An assertion F is either the membership of a subset of entities E in a given position *Pos*, $E \subseteq Pos$, the test of *Pos* for non-emptyness, $? \in Pos$, the disjunction of two assertions $F_1 \vee F_2$, their conjunction $F_1 \wedge F_2$, their exclusive or $F_1 \char`^ F_2$, or the negation of an assertion $\neg F$.

Definition 12 (Satisfaction of Assertion). *Let $v = \langle W \rhd R, I, P \rangle$ be a transition label, and F be an assertion. We write $v \models \mathsf{F}$ (read as the transition label v satisfies the assertion F) if and only if the following hold:*

$$
\begin{aligned}
v &\models E \subseteq Pos &&\textit{iff}\quad E \subseteq \mathsf{select}(v, Pos) \\
v &\models ? \in Pos &&\textit{iff}\quad \mathsf{select}(v, Pos) \neq \emptyset \\
v &\models \mathsf{F}_1 \wedge \mathsf{F}_2 &&\textit{iff}\quad v \models \mathsf{F}_1 \wedge v \models \mathsf{F}_2 \\
v &\models \mathsf{F}_1 \vee \mathsf{F}_2 &&\textit{iff}\quad v \models \mathsf{F}_1 \vee v \models \mathsf{F}_2 \\
v &\models \mathsf{F}_1 \,\hat{}\, \mathsf{F}_2 &&\textit{iff}\quad (v \models \mathsf{F}_1 \wedge v \models \neg\mathsf{F}_2) \vee (v \models \neg\mathsf{F}_1 \wedge v \models \mathsf{F}_2) \\
v &\models \neg\mathsf{F} &&\textit{iff}\quad v \not\models \mathsf{F}
\end{aligned}
$$

$$
\textit{where} \qquad \mathsf{select}(\langle W \rhd R, I, P \rangle, Pos) \triangleq
\begin{cases}
W & \textit{if } Pos = \mathcal{W} \\
R & \textit{if } Pos = \mathcal{R} \\
I & \textit{if } Pos = \mathcal{I} \\
P & \textit{if } Pos = \mathcal{P}
\end{cases}
$$

Given two transition labels v, w we write $v \equiv_\mathsf{F} w$ if $v \models \mathsf{F} \Leftrightarrow w \models \mathsf{F}$, i.e. if both v, w satisfy F or they both do not.

Example 7. Some assertions matching the queries listed in Example 6 are:

1. $\mathsf{F}_1 \triangleq \mathsf{a} \subseteq \mathcal{R}$
2. $\mathsf{F}_2 \triangleq \mathsf{ab} \subseteq \mathcal{P}$
3. $\mathsf{F}_3 \triangleq \mathsf{a} \subseteq \mathcal{W} \vee \mathsf{c} \subseteq \mathcal{W}$
4. $\mathsf{F}_4 \triangleq \mathsf{ab} \subseteq \mathcal{R} \wedge \mathsf{c} \subseteq \mathcal{I}$ checks if the reaction has been applied, while $\mathsf{F}_5 \triangleq \mathsf{a} \subseteq \mathcal{I} \vee \mathsf{b} \subseteq \mathcal{I} \vee \mathsf{c} \subseteq \mathcal{R}$ the opposite case. Alternatively, we can set $\mathsf{F}_5 \triangleq \neg\mathsf{F}_4$.

If we take the label $v = \langle \mathsf{ab} \rhd \mathsf{ab}, \mathsf{c}, \mathsf{b} \rangle$ it is immediate to check that

$$
v \models \mathsf{F}_1 \qquad v \not\models \mathsf{F}_2 \qquad v \models \mathsf{F}_3 \qquad v \models \mathsf{F}_4 \qquad v \not\models \mathsf{F}_5
$$

With respect to the assertion language proposed in our previous paper [10], the one in Definition 11 applies to a much simpler LTS, designed for Reaction Systems, while the previous one had to consider the more general kinds of labels of the multi-party process algebra cCNA, which include, e.g., the name of each reaction together with the reagents and inhibitors that provide the reason why a reaction has been applied or not. Here, reactions are anonymous, but their enabling can still be inferred from transitions labels. The main interest of this proposal is that it is directly applied to the LTS tailored for RSs.

4.2   Bio-similarity and Bio-logical Equivalence

The notion of bio-simulation builds on the above language of assertions to parameterize the induced equivalence on the property of interest. Please recall that we have defined the behaviour of the context in a non deterministic way, thus at each step, different possible sets of entities can be provided to the system and different sets of reaction can be enabled/disabled. Bio-simulation can thus be used to compare the behaviour of different systems that share some of the reactions or entities or also to compare the behaviour of the same set of reaction rules when different contexts are provided.

Definition 13 (Bio-similarity $\sim_F$ [10]**).** *Given an assertion* F, *a* bio-simu lation $\mathbf{R}_F$ *that respects* F *is a binary relation over RS processes s.t., if* P $\mathbf{R}_F$ Q *then:*

- $\forall v, P'$ *s.t.* $P \overset{v}{\Rightarrow} P'$, *then* $\exists w, Q'$ *s.t.* $Q \overset{w}{\Rightarrow} Q'$ *with* $v \equiv_F w$ *and* $P'\ \mathbf{R}_F\ Q'$.
- $\forall w, Q'$ *s.t.* $Q \overset{w}{\Rightarrow} Q'$, *then* $\exists v, P'$ *s.t.* $P \overset{v}{\Rightarrow} P'$ *with* $v \equiv_F w$ *and* $P'\ \mathbf{R}_F\ Q'$.

We let $\sim_F$ *denote the largest bio-simulation and we say that* P *is* bio-similar *to* Q, *with respect to* F, *if* P $\sim_F$ Q.

Remark 3. An alternative way to look at a bio-simulation that respects F is to define it as an ordinary bisimulation over the transition system labelled over $\{F, \neg F\}$ obtained by transforming each transition $P \overset{v}{\Rightarrow} P'$ such that $v \models F$ into $P \overset{F}{\Rightarrow} P'$ and each transition $P \overset{v}{\Rightarrow} P'$ such that $v \not\models F$ into $P \overset{\neg F}{\Rightarrow} P'$.

It can be easily shown that the identity relation is a bio-simulation and that bio-simulations are closed under (relational) inverse, composition and union and that, as a consequence, bio-similarity is an equivalence relation.

Example 8. Let us consider some variants of our working example. The behavior of $P_0 \triangleq [(ab, c, b) \mid ab.a.ac.\mathbf{0}]$ is deterministic, and its unique trace of labels is:

$$P_0 \xrightarrow{\langle ab \triangleright ab, c, b \rangle} P_1 \xrightarrow{\langle ab \triangleright ab, c, b \rangle} P_2 \xrightarrow{\langle abc \triangleright c, \emptyset, \emptyset \rangle} [(ab, c, b) \mid \mathbf{0}]$$

Instead, the behavior of $P'_0 \triangleq [(ab, c, b) \mid (ab.a.ac.\mathbf{0} + ab.a.a.\mathbf{0})]$ is non determin- istic. Now there are two possible traces of labels: the first trace is equal to the above one, and the other one follows:

$$P'_0 \xrightarrow{\langle ab \triangleright ab, c, b \rangle} P_1 \xrightarrow{\langle ab \triangleright ab, c, b \rangle} P_2 \xrightarrow{\langle abc \triangleright c, \emptyset, \emptyset \rangle} [(ab, c, b) \mid \mathbf{0}]$$
$$\xrightarrow{\langle ab \triangleright ab, c, b \rangle} P'_1 \xrightarrow{\langle ab \triangleright ab, c, b \rangle} P'_2 \xrightarrow{\langle ab \triangleright ab, c, b \rangle} [(ab, c, b) \mid b \mid \mathbf{0}]$$

Now, it is easy to check that the two processes P_0, P'_0 are not bio-similar w.r.t. the assertion $F_1 \triangleq c \in \mathcal{E}$, requiring that in the state configuration entity c is present, and are bio-similar w.r.t. the assertion $F_2 \triangleq (a \in \mathcal{R}) \frown (c \in \mathcal{R})$, requiring that either c or a are used as reactants. Hence, we write $P_0 \not\sim_{F_1} P'_0$ and $P_0 \sim_{F_2} P'_0$.

Now, we introduce a slightly modified version of the Hennessy-Milner Logic [19], called bioHML; due to the reasons we explained above, we do not want to look at the complete transition labels, thus we rely on our simple asser- tion language to make it parametric to the assertion F of interest:

Definition 14. (BioHML [10]**).** *Let* F *be an assertion, then the set of bioHML formulas* G *that respects* F *are built by the following syntax, where* $\chi \in \{F, \neg F\}$:

$$G, H ::= t \mid f \mid G \wedge G \mid G \vee G \mid \langle \chi \rangle G \mid [\chi]G$$

Remark 4. An alternative way to look at bioHML formulas is as ordinary HML formulas over the set of labels $\{F, \neg F\}$.

The semantics of a bioHML formula is the set of processes that satisfy it.

Definition 15 (Semantics of BioHML). *Let $\mathbb{P}$ denote the set of all RS processes over S. For a BioHML formula G, we define $[\![G]\!] \subseteq \mathbb{P}$ inductively on G:*

$$[\![t]\!] \triangleq \mathbb{P} \qquad [\![f]\!] \triangleq \emptyset \qquad [\![G \wedge H]\!] \triangleq [\![G]\!] \cap [\![H]\!] \qquad [\![G \vee H]\!] \triangleq [\![G]\!] \cup [\![H]\!]$$

$$[\![\langle \chi \rangle G]\!] \triangleq \{P \in \mathbb{P} : \exists \upsilon, P'. \ P \overset{\upsilon}{\Rightarrow} P' \text{ with } \upsilon \models \chi \text{ and } P' \in [\![G]\!]\}$$
$$[\![[\chi]G]\!] \triangleq \{P \in \mathbb{P} : \forall \upsilon, P'. \ P \overset{\upsilon}{\Rightarrow} P' \text{ implies } \upsilon \models \chi \text{ and } P' \in [\![G]\!]\}$$

We write $P \models G$ (P satisfies G) if and only if $P \in [\![G]\!]$.

Negation is not included in the syntax, but the converse $\overline{G}$ of a bioHML formula G can be easily defined inductively in the same way as for HML logic. We let $\mathcal{L}_F$ be the set of all bioHML formulas that respects F.

Definition 16 (Bio-logical equivalence). *We say that P, Q are bio-logically equivalent w.r.t. F, written $P \equiv_{\mathcal{L}_F} Q$, when P and Q satisfy the exactly the same bioHML formulas in $\mathcal{L}_F$, i.e. when for any $G \in \mathcal{L}_F$ we have $P \models G \Leftrightarrow Q \models G$.*

Finally, we extend the classical result establishing the correspondence between the logical equivalence induced by HML with bisimilarity for proving that bio-similarity coincides with bio-logical equivalence.

Theorem 2 (Correspondence [10]). $\sim_F \ = \ \equiv_{\mathcal{L}_F}$

Example 9. We continue by considering our running example in Example 8. There already is the evidence that the two processes $P_0 \triangleq [(ab, c, b) \mid ab.a.ac.0]$ and $P'_0 \triangleq [(ab, c, b) \mid (ab.a.ac.0 + ab.a.a.0)]$ are not bio-similar w.r.t. the assertion $F_1 \triangleq c \in \mathcal{W}$. Here, we give a bioHML formula that distinguishes P_0 and P'_0:

$$G \triangleq \langle \neg F_1 \rangle [\neg F_1] \langle \neg F_1 \rangle t.$$

In fact, G is not satisfied by P_0, written $P_0 \not\models G$, because, along the unique possible path, the labels of the first two transitions satisfy $\neg F_1$ but P_2 cannot perform any transition whose label satisfies $\neg F_1$.

Differently, $P'_0 \models G$. In fact, P'_0 can move to P'_1 with a transition whose label satisfies $\neg F_1$, then P'_1 has a unique transition to P'_2 whose label satisfies $\neg F_1$ and finally the target state P'_2 can perform a transition whose label satisfies $\neg F_1$.

5   Implementation

In Falaschi and Palma [17] we have presented some preliminary work on how to implement RS formalism in a logic programming language (Prolog). Our implementation did not aim to be highly performing. We aimed to obtain a rapid prototyping tool for implementing extensions of Reaction Systems. Our initial prototype allowed to perform finite computations on RSs, in the form of interactive processes. Here we have extended the implementation by including the more general notion of contexts, the labels and keeping track of them building corresponding LTSs. Then we have added the predicates for formulating expressions of our assertion language that acts on the transition labels. On the basis of this assertion language we have implemented a slightly modified version of the Hennessy-Milner logic to make it parametric on the specific assertion specified by the user. Our interpreter is available for download[2].

For performance reasons and in conformance with the double-arrow transition system, our implementation uses the (*InH*) rule in a *deterministic* way by maximising the sets of present inhibitors and lacking reagents in the current computation. This improves the efficiency of the tool. We have run and checked the examples in this paper, by using our interpreter. As explained in the online instructions, the tool can be customised by instantiating a few predicates providing the Reaction System specification and a BioHML formula to be verified.

6   Two Extensions

Here we present two extensions: a numeric extension that takes into account the number of times an entity is used as a reactant in a single transition; an extension that introduces an operator for letting two RSs be *connected*.

Reactant Occurrences
The first idea is to introduce some naive measure for the number of entities that are needed by the reactions. Now, we assume that the number associated to entities in the sets R (reactants) and P (products) are the stoichiometric numbers, as specified in the corresponding biochemical equation. This amounts to use multisets instead of sets (for R and P) within the labels. The set I (of inhibitors) remains a simple set. At the level of notation, we write a multiset as a formal sum $\bigoplus_{a \in S} n_a a$, where $n_a \in \mathbb{N}$ is the number of occurrences of a. For simplicity, we write just a instead of $1a$ and we omit any term of the form $0a$. For example, the multiset $2a \oplus b$ has two instances of a and one of b. Overloading the notation we use $\cup$ as multiset union, i.e.

$$\left(\bigoplus_{a \in S} n_a a\right) \cup \left(\bigoplus_{a \in S} m_a a\right) = \bigoplus_{a \in S} (n_a + m_a)a$$

If $R = \bigoplus_{a \in S} n_a a$ we let $R(a) = n_a$.

Similarly, we want to use multisets also for the contexts, but in this case we want the possibility to parameterize the context w.r.t. the number of entities it provides. To this purpose, fixed a finite set $X = \{x_1, ..., x_n\}$ of variables, we introduce some linear expressions of the form $e = \sum_{i=1}^{n} k_i x_i + h$ with coefficients $k_i, h \in \mathbb{N}$, such that a context C associates to each entity a a linear expression e_a and not just a number. Thus we write a context C as a formal sum $C = \bigoplus_{a \in S} e_a a$.

A multiset is just a particular case of the above expression where all variable coefficients are 0. For example, we can let $C = (x+y)\mathsf{a} \oplus (x+1)\mathsf{b}$. The union of contexts is then defined as follows

$$\bigoplus_{\mathsf{a} \in S} e_\mathsf{a}^1 \mathsf{a} \cup \bigoplus_{\mathsf{a} \in S} e_\mathsf{a}^2 \mathsf{a} = \bigoplus_{\mathsf{a} \in S} (e_\mathsf{a}^1 + e_\mathsf{a}^2)\mathsf{a}$$

We assume that variables in X can only range over positive values, so that if $e_\mathsf{a} \neq 0$ then a is present in $\bigoplus_{\mathsf{a} \in S} e_\mathsf{a}\mathsf{a}$.

In the SOS rules we need to use the requirements $(W \cup R) \cap I = \emptyset$ and $R \subseteq W$. They are intended to be satisfied at the qualitative level, not necessarily at the quantitative one. Correspondingly, the disjointness condition $(W \cup R) \cap I = \emptyset$ is satisfied when $\forall \mathsf{a} \in I.\ (W \cup R)(\mathsf{a}) = 0$, and the inclusion condition $R \subseteq W$ is satisfied when $\forall \mathsf{a} \in S.\ R(\mathsf{a}) \neq 0 \Rightarrow W(\mathsf{a}) \neq 0$. Our new transition labels differ from the ones in Fig. 1 just because R, P, and W are now multisets. We keep the same SOS rules as before.

The advantage is that to each transition $\mathsf{P} \xrightarrow{\langle W \triangleright R, I, P \rangle} \mathsf{P}'$ we can now assign a system of linear inequalities: $\forall \mathsf{a} \in S.\ R(\mathsf{a}) \leq W(\mathsf{a})$, where $R(\mathsf{a}) \in \mathbb{N}$ and $W(\mathsf{a})$ is an expression. The aim is to estimate, with no computational effort, the *relative quantities* of biological material which should be provided to the system to reach a desired configuration. This could be helpful during the setting phase of an *in vitro* experiment to avoid over-use of biological material, given its high cost. Please note that the qualitative nature of RS is unchanged, we only add some extra information that we elaborate by manipulating transition labels, only. Here we give an intuition with a short example.

Example 10. Let us consider the chemical reactions in Table 3 in Azimi et al. [2], in particular reactions (*i*) and (*vii*); we will use their formalization in the syntax of RS, by keeping the stoichiometric numbers:

$$a_1 \triangleq (\{(\mathsf{hsf}, 3)\}, \{\mathsf{d_l}\}, \{\mathsf{hsf_3}\}) \qquad a_2 \triangleq (\{\mathsf{hsp}, \mathsf{hsf_3}\}, \{\mathsf{d_l}\}, \{\mathsf{hsp{:}hsf}, (\mathsf{hsf}, 2)\})$$

Reaction a_1 requires three copies of the entity hsf, while a_2 produces two copies of hsf. We assume that the context initially provides the set $C \triangleq x\mathsf{hsf} \oplus \mathsf{hsp} \oplus \mathsf{hsf_3}$ and then it provides the empty set, i.e. it is defined as $\mathsf{K} \triangleq C.\emptyset.\mathbf{0}$. The resulting system can only execute two transitions: in the first transition both reactions a_1 and a_2 are applied, in the second transition only reaction a_1 is applied:

$$[\mathsf{K}|a_1|a_2] \xrightarrow{\langle C \triangleright R, I, P \rangle} [P|\emptyset.\mathbf{0}|a_1|a_2] \xrightarrow{\langle P \triangleright R', I', P' \rangle} [P'|\mathbf{0}|a_1|a_2]$$

where $R = 3\mathsf{hsf} \oplus \mathsf{hsp} \oplus \mathsf{hsf_3} \quad I = \{\mathsf{d_l}\} \qquad P = \mathsf{hsf_3} \oplus \mathsf{hsp{:}hsf} \oplus 2\mathsf{hsf}$
$R' = 3\mathsf{hsf} \qquad\qquad\qquad I' = \{\mathsf{hsp}, \mathsf{d_l}\} \quad P' = \mathsf{hsf_3}$

Now, from the first transition we extract the requirement $R(\mathsf{hsf}) = 3 \leq C(\mathsf{hsf}) = x$, while from the second transition we get $R'(\mathsf{hsf}) = 3 \leq P(\mathsf{hsf}) = 2$. If we would wanted a quantitative estimate of need of entity hsf, this comparison would reveal that the production of hsf is not sufficient to trigger the second reaction.

$$\frac{P_1 \xrightarrow{\langle W_1 \rhd R_1, I_1, P_1 \rangle} P \quad P_2 \xrightarrow{\langle W_2 \rhd R_2, I_2, P_2 \rangle} [M]}{P_1 \overset{L}{\Mapsto} P_2 \xrightarrow{\langle W_1 \cup W_2 \rhd R_1 \cup R_2, I_1 \cup I_2, P_1 \cup P_2 \rangle} P \overset{L}{\Mapsto} [M | (L \cap P_1)]} \quad (Lnk)$$

Fig. 2. SOS semantics rule for the connector operator

The Connector Operator. In Bodei et al. [9] and Brodo et al. [10] we have presented the encoding of RS into the link-calculus and discussed how to connect two encoded RS such that some of the entities produced by one RS are provided to the second one, similarly to what has been done in Bottoni et al. [7]. Thus we introduce a "connector", written as $P_1 \overset{L}{\Mapsto} P_2$ 2: when the RS process P_1 produces entities in the set L, these entities are available, at the next step, as reactants to the continuations of both RS processes. When $L = \emptyset$, there cannot be any exchange of entities and P_1 and P_2 run in parallel.

7   Conclusion and Future Work

We have presented an SOS semantics for the Reaction Systems that generates a labelled transition system. We have revised RSs as processes, formulating a set of ad-hoc inference rules. Our flexible framework allows one to add new operators in a natural way. The transition labels add expressivity at the computation allowing for additional analysis, as we did in Sect. 4. In Sect. 5 we have described a preliminary interpreter in logic programming which implements the verification of BioHML formulas on computations of RS processes with nondeterministic contexts in our framework. As future work we plan to define SOS semantics for other synchronous rewrite-rule systems to define a uniform computational framework. We plan to improve our implementation including its functionalities, interface, scalability and usability, for the analysis of large case studies. We want to study the relation to analysis techniques [13,15,16].

Acknowledgments. We thank the anonymous reviewers for their detailed and very useful criticisms and recommendations that helped us to improve our paper.

References

1. Azimi, S.: Steady states of constrained reaction systems. Theor. Comput. Sci. **701**(C), 20–26 (2017). https://doi.org/10.1016/j.tcs.2017.03.047
2. Azimi, S., Iancu, B., Petre, I.: Reaction system models for the heat shock response. Fundam. Inf. **131**(3–4), 299–312 (2014). https://doi.org/10.3233/FI-2014-1016
3. Barbuti, R., Gori, R., Levi, F., Milazzo, P.: Investigating dynamic causalities in reaction systems. Theor. Comput. Sci. **623**, 114–145 (2016). https://doi.org/10.1016/j.tcs.2015.11.041
4. Barbuti, R., Maggiolo-Schettini, A., Milazzo, P., Troina, A.: Bisimulations in calculi modelling membranes. Form. Asp. Comput. **20**(4), 351–377 (2008). https://doi.org/10.1007/s00165-008-0071-x

5. Bodei, C., Brodo, L., Bruni, R.: A formal approach to open multiparty interactions. Theor. Comput. Sci. **763**, 38–65 (2019). https://doi.org/10.1016/j.tcs.2019.01.033
6. Bodei, C., Brodo, L., Bruni, R.: The link-calculus for open multiparty interactions. Inf. Comput. **275**, 104587 (2020). https://doi.org/10.1016/j.ic.2020.104587
7. Bottoni, P., Labella, A., Rozenberg, G.: Networks of reaction systems. Int. J. Found. Comput. Sci. **31**, 53–71 (2020). https://doi.org/10.1142/S0129054120400043
8. Brijder, R., Ehrenfeucht, A., Main, M., Rozenberg, G.: A tour of reaction systems. Int. J. Found. Comput. Sci. **22**(07), 1499–1517 (2011). https://doi.org/10.1142/S0129054111008842
9. Brodo, L., Bruni, R., Falaschi, M.: Enhancing reaction systems: a process algebraic approach. In: Alvim, M.S., Chatzikokolakis, K., Olarte, C., Valencia, F. (eds.) The Art of Modelling Computational Systems: A Journey from Logic and Concurrency to Security and Privacy. LNCS, vol. 11760, pp. 68–85. Springer, Cham (2019). https://doi.org/10.1007/978-3-030-31175-9_5
10. Brodo, L., Bruni, R., Falaschi, M.: A process algebraic approach to reaction systems. Theor. Comput. Sci. (2020). https://doi.org/10.1016/j.tcs.2020.09.001. In Press
11. Cardelli, L., Gordon, A.D.: Mobile ambients. Theor. Comput. Sci. **240**(1), 177–213 (2000). https://doi.org/10.1016/S0304-3975(99)00231-5
12. Cardelli, L., Tribastone, M., Tschaikowski, M., Vandin, A.: Forward and backward bisimulations for chemical reaction networks. In: CONCUR 2015, vol. 42, pp. 226–239. Schloss Dagstuhl Publ. (2015). https://doi.org/10.4230/LIPIcs.CONCUR.2015.226
13. Chiarugi, D., Falaschi, M., Olarte, C., Palamidessi, C.: Compositional modelling of signalling pathways in timed concurrent constraint programming. In: BCB 2010, pp. 414–417. ACM (2010). https://doi.org/10.1145/1854776.1854843
14. Corolli, L., Maj, C., Marinia, F., Besozzi, D., Mauri, G.: An excursion in reaction systems: from computer science to biology. Theor. Comput. Sci. **454**, 95–108 (2012). https://doi.org/10.1016/j.tcs.2012.04.003
15. Falaschi, M., Olarte, C., Palamidessi, C.: Abstract interpretation of temporal concurrent constraint programs. Theory Pract. Logic Program. **15**(3), 312–357 (2015). https://doi.org/10.1017/S1471068413000641
16. Falaschi, M., Olarte, C., Palamidessi, C.: A framework for abstract interpretation of timed concurrent constraint programs. In: PPDP 2009. pp. 207–218. ACM (2009). https://doi.org/10.1145/1599410.1599436
17. Falaschi, M., Palma, G.: A logic programming approach to reaction systems. In: DIP 2020. OASIcs, vol. 86, pp. 6:1–6:15. Schloss Dagstuhl-Leibniz-Zentrum für Informatik (2020). https://doi.org/10.4230/OASIcs.Gabbrielli.6
18. Gordon, A., Cardelli, L.: Equational properties of mobile ambients. Math. Struct. Comput. Sci. **13**(3), 371–408 (2003). https://doi.org/10.1017/S0960129502003742
19. Hennessy, M., Milner, R.: On observing nondeterminism and concurrency. In: de Bakker, J., van Leeuwen, J. (eds.) ICALP 1980. LNCS, vol. 85, pp. 299–309. Springer, Heidelberg (1980). https://doi.org/10.1007/3-540-10003-2_79
20. Hillston, J.: A compositional approach to performance modelling. Ph.D. thesis, University of Edinburgh, UK (1994). http://hdl.handle.net/1842/15027
21. Kleijn, J., Koutny, M., Mikulski, Ł, Rozenberg, G.: Reaction systems, transition systems, and equivalences. In: Böckenhauer, H.-J., Komm, D., Unger, W. (eds.) Adventures Between Lower Bounds and Higher Altitudes. LNCS, vol. 11011, pp. 63–84. Springer, Cham (2018). https://doi.org/10.1007/978-3-319-98355-4_5

22. Milner, R. (ed.): A Calculus of Communicating Systems. LNCS, vol. 92. Springer, Heidelberg (1980). https://doi.org/10.1007/3-540-10235-3
23. Milner, R., Sangiorgi, D.: Barbed bisimulation. In: Kuich, W. (ed.) ICALP 1992. LNCS, vol. 623, pp. 685–695. Springer, Heidelberg (1992). https://doi.org/10.1007/3-540-55719-9_114
24. Okubo, F., Yokomori, T.: The computational capability of chemical reaction automata. Nat. Comput. **15**(2), 215–224 (2015). https://doi.org/10.1007/s11047-015-9504-7
25. Plotkin, G.D.: A structural approach to operational semantics. Technical report DAIMI FN-19, Computer Science Department, Aarhus University (1981)
26. Plotkin, G.D.: An operational semantics for CSP. In: IFIP Working Conference on Formal Description of Programming Concepts - II, North-Holland, pp. 199–226 (1982)
27. Plotkin, G.D.: A structural approach to operational semantics. J. Log. Algebraic Methods Program. **60–61**, 17–139 (2004). https://doi.org/10.1016/j.jlap.2004.05.001
28. Sangiorgi, D.: Introduction to Bisimulation and Coinduction. Cambridge University Press, USA (2011). https://doi.org/10.1017/CBO9780511777110

Practical Idiomatic Considerations for Checkable Meta-logic in Experimental Functional Programming

Baltasar Trancón y Widemann$^{(\boxtimes)}$ and Markus Lepper

semantics GmbH, Berlin, Germany
baltasar@trancon.de

Abstract. Implementing a complex concept as an executable model in a strongly typed, purely functional language hits a sweet spot between mere simulation and formal specification. For research and education it is often desirable to enrich the algorithmic code with meta-logical annotations, variously embodied as assertions, theorems or test cases. Checking frameworks use the inherent logical power of the functional paradigm to approximate theorem proving by heuristic testing. Here we propose several novel idioms to enhance the practical expressivity of checking, namely meta-language marking, nominal axiomatics, and constructive existentials. All of these are formulated in literate Haskell'98 with some common language extensions. Their use and impact are illustrated by application to a realistic modeling problem.

Keywords: Executable modeling · Property-based testing · Reified logic

1 Introduction

This paper discusses general programming methodology in terms of a particular implementation in Haskell. Thus it is provided as a literate Haskell [10] program.[1]

1.1 Proving and Checking

Purely functional programming has arguably a friendlier relationship to meta-logic, the discipline of formal reasoning about program properties, than conventional state-based paradigms [1]. This has been exploited in a number of ways that differ greatly in their pragmatic context.

At one end of the spectrum, strongly normalizing languages and the types-as-propositions approach, ultimately based on the Brouwer–Heyting–Kolmogorov interpretation of constructive logic, have led to the unification of algorithmic

---

[1] A full and self-contained source archive for practical evaluation is publicly available at http://bandm.eu/download/purecheck/.

© Springer Nature Switzerland AG 2021
M. Hanus and C. Sacerdoti Coen (Eds.): WFLP 2020, LNCS 12560, pp. 22–38, 2021.
https://doi.org/10.1007/978-3-030-75333-7_2

programming and constructive *theorem proving*. The practice has evolved from basic models such as the Calculus of Constructions [6] to full-blown languages and interactive programming environments such as Agda [9]. The basic approach is that a program is statically validated with respect to a type signature that encodes the desired meta-logical property, if and only if it truly possesses that property. This approach does evidently not scale to Turing-complete languages.[2] Thus, for meta-logic over complete programming languages, it is not sufficient to demonstrate *inhabitation* of a type to obtain a proof, but it must also stand the test of successful *evaluation*.

At the other end of the spectrum, freedom from side effects allows for liberally sprinkling program code with *online assertions*, that is, computations whose values the program depends on not for its outcome, but for ensuring its correct operation. Some care must be exercised when timing and strictness details matter [2], but otherwise the technique is just as powerful as for conventional programming paradigms [4], minus the need for a pure assertion sublanguage.

The middle ground is covered by *offline checking*[3], that is, evaluation of meta-logical properties as a separate mode of program execution. Offline checking is of course less rigorous than theorem proving, and may involve incomplete and heuristic reasoning procedures. On the other hand, it is more abstract and static than online assertions; thus cases that are not reached during online evaluation can be covered, and the checking effort can be shifted to convenient points in the software lifecycle. Offline checking fills the same role as conventional *unit testing* procedures, although the focus is a bit different: checking purely functional programs is commonly both simpler in control, due to the lack of state of the unit under test that needs to be set up and observed, and more complex in data, due to the pervasiveness of higher-order functions.

There are various popular offline checking frameworks for functional programming languages, such as QuickCheck, (Lazy) SmallCheck, SmartCheck, ScalaCheck or PropEr, and we assume the reader is familiar with their general design and operation, for instance with the seminal QuickCheck [3] for Haskell.

The contribution of the present paper is a collection of three novel and experimental idioms for offline checking. The definitions and an example application are given in the following two main sections, respectively. These features have been implemented in Haskell for PureCheck, but are theoretically compatible with other frameworks and host languages.

1.2 Executable Modeling

The field of executable modeling, that is, the construction of experimental programs that embody theoretical concepts of systems and processes, and imbue

---

[2] Consider the "constructive" logical reading of the type of a generic recursion operator, $(\alpha \rightarrow \alpha) \rightarrow \alpha$; it says literally that *begging the question*, $\alpha \rightarrow \alpha$, is a valid proof method for any proposition α.

[3] Thus named here for clear contrast with the alternatives, but largely synonymous with *property-based testing* [7].

them with practically observable behavior, poses specific challenges. In particular, some mechanism is needed to *validate* the implementation, that is, establish trust in its faithful representation of the concepts under study. Since executable models are designed to exceed behavioral a-priori intuition (otherwise their content were trivial) [5], it is intrinsically hard to differentiate bugs from features.

In a naive idealistic sense, model programs should be derived and proved rigorously. However, that presupposes a complete, computable and operationalized theory. For the two scenarios where a theory exists but is not fully operationalized, and where models are used *inductively* as approximations to a future theory, we consider less rigorous approaches, and offline checking in particular, the more viable validation procedure. It may even be educational to both check and run models that behave evidently wrong.

1.3   The PureCheck Framework

The checking idioms to be proposed in the following have been developed in the context of an experimental checking framework, PureCheck, implemented as a plain Haskell library. The design of PureCheck largely follows the paradigm of popular frameworks such as QuickCheck [3] or SmallCheck [11], with some notable deviations.

Like other frameworks, PureCheck leverages the internal logical language of functional programming, and type-directed generation of test data for universal propositions. PureCheck prioritizes purity and non-strictness; text execution is rigidly non-monadic, and thus equally suitable for both offline checks and online assertions. Unlike QuickCheck, test data are generated by deterministic rather than randomized combinatorial procedures. Unlike SmallCheck, sample sizes can be bounded precisely, without risk of combinatorial explosion. Test data sets are pessimistically assumed to be possibly insufficient, and thus the direction of logical approximation is significant; evaluation may yield false positives, resulting from undiscovered counterexamples, but never false negatives.

PureCheck Basics. At the heart of the framework is an encapsulation for heuristic checks.

newtype *Check* = *Check* { *perform* :: *Int* → *Bool* }

The heuristic is parameterized with an *Int* called the *confidence* parameter. Because of monotonicity, higher values may require more computational effort, but can only improve the test accuracy by eliminating more false positives.

The propositions that can be encapsulated in this way come in various shapes; thus we define a type class with an ad-hoc polymorphic encapsulation operation.

class *Checkable* α **where** *check* :: *Meta* α → *Check*

The wrapper *Meta* should be ignored for now; it shall be discussed in due detail in the following section. The base case is a propositional constant.

instance *Checkable Bool* **where** *check* (*Meta b*) = *Check* (*const b*)

Checks bear the obvious conjunctive monoid structure. Since the aggregate confidence in the truth of a conjunction can be no higher than the individual confidence in any of its clauses, the parameter is copied clause-wise.

instance *Monoid Check* **where**
  mempty   = *Check* ($\lambda n \to True$)
  mappend (*Check c*) (*Check d*) = *Check* ($\lambda n \to c\ n \wedge d\ n$)
 instance *Checkable* () **where** *check* (*Meta* ()) = *mempty*
 instance (*Checkable* α, *Checkable* β) $\Rightarrow$ *Checkable* (α, β) **where**
   check (*Meta* (*p, q*)) = *check* (*Meta p*) '*mappend*' *check* (*Meta q*)
 instance (*Checkable* α) $\Rightarrow$ *Checkable* [α] **where**
   check (*Meta ps*) = *mconcat* (*map* (*check* $\circ$ *Meta*) *ps*)

For quantified universals, a generator for representative samples of the argument space is required. The confidence parameter is taken as the recommended maximum sample size (unlike SmallCheck, where the parameter is a *depth* to be exhausted, such that sample size may be only exponentially related). Unlike in the conjunctive case, nested universal quantifiers are not simply dealt with recursively. Instead, it is recommended to use uncurried forms quantified over tuples to ensure proper weight-balancing between argument samples.

checkWith :: *Generator* $\alpha \to Meta$ ($\alpha \to Bool$) $\to Check$
checkWith g (*Meta p*) = *Check* ($\lambda n \to all\ p$ (*generate g n*))
 instance (*Some* α) $\Rightarrow$ *Checkable* ($\alpha \to Bool$) **where**
   check = *checkWith some*

Test data generators are wrapped pure functions, and thus deterministic in the size parameter n. Useful generators return at most (preferably approximately) n elements (preferably distinct and with commensurate internal variety).

newtype *Generator* α = *Generator* { *generate* :: *Int* $\to$ [α] }

A type class provides default generators for its instance types.

class *Some* α **where** *some* :: *Generator* α

Generators for simple types are straightforward, for instance:

instance *Some Bool* **where**
  some = *Generator* $ *flip take* [*False, True*]

Generator combinators for complex types need to consider the issues of weight balancing between dimensions and of infinite enumerations; the details are out of scope here.[4]

---

[4] Implementations can be found in the full source.

2   Proposed Idioms

2.1   Meta-language Marking

The principle of types as propositions in a functional programming language is a two-sided coin. On the upside, the internal logical language is automatically consistent with the language semantics, and quite expressive. On the downside, the expressive power of advanced abstractions such as higher-order functions and polymorphism is a bit too much for the logical needs of the average user. Unrestrained use can make the meta-logical aspects of the codebase overwhelmingly hard to both write and read.[5]

We propose that, for both education and engineering, it is a wise move to delimit the parts of the codebase that are intended as meta-logical vocabulary explicitly. To this end, we introduce a generic wrapper type.

data $Meta\ \alpha = Meta\ \{reflect :: \alpha\}$

Then the codebase is manifestly stratified into four layers:

Operational definitions do *not* use the *Meta* type/value constructor.
Assertive definitions use the *Meta* constructor in *root* position.
Tactical definitions use the *Meta* constructor in *non-root* position.
Transcendent definitions are polymorphic over a type (constructor) variable that admits some *Meta* α (or *Meta* itself, respectively) as an *instance*.

The effect of this stratified marking discipline is that, contrarily to the pathological *foldl* example presented above, the intented reading of type signatures becomes clear. For instance:

- *Meta Bool* is the type of atomic assertive meta-expressions that are expected to evaluate straightforwardly to *True*; definitions of this type incur a *singleton* static checking obligation, that is a *test case*.
- *Meta Int* is a type of meta-expressions without a truth-value, let alone an expected one; definitions of this type incur no static checking obligation.
- *Meta* $(A \rightarrow Bool)$[6] is the type of quantified assertive meta-expressions that are expected to evaluate to *True* for all parameter values of type A; definitions of this type incur a static checking obligation for *some* values (preferably a representative set).
- $A \rightarrow Meta\ Bool$ is the type of tactics that can construct such assertions from parameter values of type A; definitions of this type incur *no* static checking obligation, but may implement an aspect of a *test strategy*.
- *Meta* $A \rightarrow Meta\ B$ is the type of tactics that can transform an assertion of type A to an assertion of type B; definitions of this type incur no checking obligation, but may implement an aspect of a test strategy.

---

[5] The reader is invited to contemplate for example the variety of possible higher-order logical meanings of the following specialization of a well-known Haskell Prelude function: $foldl :: (Foldable\ \tau) \Rightarrow (Bool \rightarrow \alpha \rightarrow Bool) \rightarrow Bool \rightarrow \tau\ \alpha \rightarrow Bool$.

[6] Note the discourse-level meta-variable A for a monomorphic Haskell type, instead of an object-level type variable α.

- *Meta A* → *Bool* is the type of tactics that can evaluate a meta-property of an assertion of type *A*; definitions of this type incur no checking obligation, but may implement an aspect of a test strategy.
- *Meta* (α → *Bool*) → *Meta* ([α] → *Bool*) is the type of parametrically polymorphic predicate transformers that lifts an assertion meta-expression quantified over an arbitrary element type α to one quantified over the corresponding list type [α].

Note that transport of operational subexpressions into the meta-logical layer is the simple matter of a *Meta* data constructor. By contrast, the reverse transport using the projection *reflect* is discouraged except for certain idiomatic cases.

Evidently level marking makes no contribution to algorithmic computations. That it is pragmatically valuable documentation nevertheless is demonstrated by the explicit meta-logical universal quantifier:

foreach :: (α → *Meta* β) → *Meta* (α → β)
foreach f = *Meta* (λx → *reflect* (*f x*))

If *f* is a predicate that is used pointwise to form meta-expressions, then *foreach f* is a singular meta-expression that quantifies over all points. For example,

Meta ∘ *even* :: *Int* → *Meta Bool*

is clearly a predicate intended to be used pointwise since the alternative reading, "all integers are even", is blatantly false. By contrast,

foreach (*Meta* ∘ *even* ∘ (∗2)) :: *Meta* (*Int* → *Bool*)

is a (true) universal assertion quantified over all (non-⊥) values of type *Int*.

As a more relevant example, consider a preorder of meta-logical interest, say a semantic approximation relation, on some data type *A*.

($\sqsubseteq$) :: *A* → *A* → *Meta Bool*

This is directly usable as a binary predicate that characterizes the relationship of two particular elements. By converting one quantifier, we obtain a unary predicate that characterizes a particular element as globally minimal:

minimal :: *A* → *Meta* (*A* → *Bool*)
minimal x = *foreach* (*x* $\sqsubseteq$)

By converting the other quantifier also, we obtain a nullary predicate that characterizes the preorder as trivial:

trivial :: *Meta* (*A* → *A* → *Bool*)
trivial = *foreach minimal*

The final conversion to the recommended uncurried type *Meta* ((*A, A*) → *Bool*) can be performed explicitly (left as an exercise to the reader), or implicitly by a suitable instance of *Checkable*.

This style ensures that higher-order functions and meta-logical reading are orthogonal means of expressivity.

All checking ultimately involves the evaluation of an expression of type *Meta Bool*. The denotational semantics of this Haskell type has four meaningful values, namely:

Value	Verdict: The checked property	Issue type
Meta True	...holds	—
Meta False	...does not hold	logical falsehood
Meta $\perp$	...cannot be decided	logical error
$\perp$	...cannot be stated	tactical error

Semantic $\perp$ values occuring intermediately, such as in tactical computations or test data generation, are not constrained by our framework. To the contrary, non-strictness can be exploited in useful ways to manipulate complex meta-logical constructs. For instance, consider a form of bounded quantification, where an explicit sample generator is provided:

data *For* α β = *For* { *bound* :: *Generator* α, *body* :: $\alpha \to \beta$ }
instance *Checkable* (*For* α *Bool*) **where**
  check (*Meta* (*For* g p)) = *checkWith* g (*Meta* p)

Nested bounded quantifications of the form *For* g ($\lambda x \to$ *For* h ($\lambda y \to p$)) cannot be merged or transposed straightforwardly, because a lambda abstraction intervenes. However, semantics can be exploited if h is independent of, and thus non-strict in x.

qmerge :: *For* α (*For* β γ) $\to$ *For* (α, β) γ
qmerge (*For* g k) = **let** $h = bound$ (k $\perp$)
                  in *For* (*gpair* g h) ($\lambda(x, y) \to body$ (k x) y)

Here *gpair* forms a Cartesian sample product for marginal generators g and h.[7]

2.2   Nominal Axiomatics

In a types-as-propositions approach to meta-logic of functional programs, a property of interest is encoded as a dependent type, and holds if the type can be demonstrated to be inhabited in a constructive semantics.

By contrast, checking approaches are *empirical*: Properties of interest are tested by computable functions, and thus collapse to the result type *Bool*, of which only the value *True* is accepted. A seemingly trivial, but practically significant consequence is that type signatures are not helpful to prevent accidental confusion of structurally similar properties.

---

[7] The implementation of *gpair* is explained in detail in the full source.

This issue is compounded, quite paradoxically, by abstraction mechanisms. Often a proposition can be stated in concise generic form by abstraction from values, types or type class instances. The actual checking then operates on a particular concretization (by application in the former and type inference in the latter two cases, respectively).

In this context, misreference or omission errors are easy to commit and hard to detect. Hence it is of some practical importance to organize the meta-logical propositions attached to a particular reusable program part clearly and accountably. Adequate solutions appear to depend heavily on the programming style; the following guidelines should thus be understood as both flexible and incomplete.

Theory Type Classes. A substantial part of model-ish functional programs is about the algebra of data structures. For structures organized in the idiomatic Haskell way as type classes, the associated meta-logic can conveniently be organized as a companion type class with default implementations. This bundles the laws and makes them accessible to simultaneous instantiation, and to automatic enumeration via meta-programming (which is not discussed here).

For example, consider the implied laws of the Prelude type class *Monoid*:

```
class (Monoid α) ⇒ MonoidTheory α where
   monoid_left_unit :: (Eq α) ⇒ Meta (α → Bool)
   monoid_left_unit = Meta (λx → mempty ◇ x ≡ x)

   monoid_right_unit :: (Eq α) ⇒ Meta (α → Bool)
   monoid_right_unit = Meta (λx → x ◇ mempty ≡ x)

   monoid_assoc :: (Eq α) ⇒ Meta ((α, α, α) → Bool)
   monoid_assoc = Meta (λ(x, y, z)   → (x ◇ y) ◇ z ≡ x ◇ (y ◇ z))
```

Note that there is some design leeway with respect to type class contexts. For illustration, we have distinguished here between the "essential" context *Monoid* α, declared on the type class and hence detected upon instantiation, and the "accidental" context *Eq* α, declared on each method and hence detected upon use. The distinction may or may not be ambiguous in practice, however.

Type-Level Ad-Hoc Programming. For more ad-hoc data structures, where operations are not organized as methods of a type class, but rather passed explicitly to higher-order functions, or where extra laws are assumed locally, a likewise looser style of meta-logic appears more adequate. Fortunately, there is no need to relinquish the assistance of the Haskell type and context checker altogether. A type class can be used to map symbolic names of laws, defined as constructors of ad-hoc datatypes, to their logical content.

```
class Axiom α π | α → π where axiomatic :: α → Meta π
```

In line with the previous example, an extra law that is not reflected by a Haskell type class can be defined and made referable by a singleton polymorphic datatype.

data $MonoidCommute\ \alpha = MonoidCommute$
instance $(Monoid\ \alpha,\ Eq\ \alpha) \Rightarrow$
   $Axiom\ (MonoidCommute\ \alpha)\ ((\alpha, \alpha) \to Bool)$ **where**
  $axiomatic\ MonoidCommute = Meta\ (\lambda(x, y) \to x \diamond y \equiv y \diamond x)$

A law for an ad-hoc data structure with explicitly passed operations is analogously defined as a record-like datatype. For instance consider a law of monoid actions (also cf. the type signature of *foldl*):

type $RAction\ \alpha\ \beta = \beta \to \alpha \to \beta$
data $RActionUnit\ \alpha\ \beta = RActionUnit\ (RAction\ \alpha\ \beta)$
instance $(Monoid\ \alpha,\ Eq\ \beta) \Rightarrow$
   $Axiom\ (RActionUnit\ \alpha\ \beta)\ (\beta \to Bool)$ **where**
  $axiomatic\ (RActionUnit\ (\lhd)) = Meta\ (\lambda x \to x \lhd mempty \equiv x)$
data $RActionCompose\ \alpha\ \beta = RActionCompose\ (RAction\ \alpha\ \beta)$
instance $(Monoid\ \alpha,\ Eq\ \beta) \Rightarrow$
   $Axiom\ (RActionCompose\ \alpha\ \beta)\ (\beta \to \alpha \to \alpha \to Bool)$ **where**
  $axiomatic\ (RActionCompose\ (\lhd)) = Meta\ (\lambda x\ y\ z \to x \lhd (y \diamond z) \equiv (x \lhd y) \lhd z)$

For richer classification, type subclasses can be used to create ad-hoc subsets of "axiom space". This both adds to the documentation value of actual meta-level code, and protects against misuse of tactics. For instance, consider a class of *Int*-parameterized meta-level expressions that need only be checked for non-negative parameter values:

class $(Axiom\ \alpha\ (Int \to \beta)) \Rightarrow NonNegAxiom\ \alpha\ \beta$

This subclass can be accompanied with an axiom-level operator, by giving a constructor type and corresponding operational lifting:

data $NonNeg\ \alpha = NonNeg\ \alpha$
instance $(NonNegAxiom\ \alpha\ \beta) \Rightarrow Axiom\ (NonNeg\ \alpha)\ (Int \to \beta)$ **where**
  $axiomatic\ (NonNeg\ a) = Meta\ (reflect\ (axiomatic\ a) \circ abs)$

The restriction of the instance context to the subclass *NonNegAxiom* ensures application of this (generally unsafe) tactic only to axioms that have an explicit membership declaration, which can serve as an anchor for individual justification, be it prose reasoning or checkable lemmata.

2.3   Constructive Existentials

The natural logical reading of the type operator $(\to)$ is universal quantification. But existential quantification also often arises in formulas, either explicitly or by DeMorgan's laws, when universal quantification occurs in a negative position, such as under negation or on the left hand side of implication.

Checking existential quantification with the same sampling-based mechanisms as universal quantification would break the monotonicity of heuristics:

For universal quantifiers, only false positives can arise if counterexamples exist but are not present in the sample. As such, confidence can only improve when the sample size is increased. By contrast, for existential quantifiers, false negatives can arise when witness exist but are not present in the sample. False negatives are at best annoying when they occur at the top level and raise false alarms, but at worst, when arising negatively nested in a complex formula, they can make overall confidence *decrease* with increasing sample size.

Therefore we propose to treat existential quantification as entirely distinct, and in the true spirit of constructive logic, by effective Skolemization. To make an existential assertion checkable, a witness must be provided in an effectively computable fashion.

> **class** *Witness* α β | $\alpha \to \beta$ **where** *witness* :: $\alpha \to$ *Maybe* β

Here α is a data type that encodes the meta-logical predicate to quantify, and β is the domain to quantify over. The ad-hoc polymorphic operation *witness* may yield *Nothing* to indicate that no witness could be found for the given predicate instance. The extraction of a witness can then be composed with a payload predicate to form bounded existential quantifications.

> *exists* :: (*Witness* α β) $\Rightarrow \alpha \to (\beta \to Bool) \to Bool$
> *exists p q* = **case** *witness p* **of**
>   *Just x* $\to q\ x$
>   *Nothing* $\to$ *False*

Note that the *exists* itself quantifier is not marked with *Meta*, as it is perfectly suitable for use in the operational codebase layer as well.

> *existsSome* :: (*Witness* α β) $\Rightarrow \alpha \to Bool$
> *existsSome p* = *exists p* (*const True*)
>
> *existsOrVacuous* :: (*Witness* α β) $\Rightarrow \alpha \to (\beta \to Bool) \to Bool$
> *existsOrVacuous p q* = **case** *witness p* **of**
>   *Just x* $\to q\ x$
>   *Nothing* $\to$ *True*

3   Example Application: Theory of (String) Patches

We illustrate the use and impact of the checking idioms described above by applying them to a conceptual problem arising from real-world software engineering research: An algebraic theory of compositional patching.

The generic level of the theory studies non-Abelian groups of patches acting partially on some arbitrary state space. As a simple but illuminating example instance, we consider the particular space of ordinary character strings, and a group generated by atomic *insert* and *delete* operations and their evident semantics. Establishing the decidability of the word problem of this group is already a non-trivial modeling task, where the expressivity gained by our proposed checking idioms comes in handy for rapid validation.

3.1   Group Words and Actions

The theoretical background for a type of patches π is its (right) action, a partial function on some state space σ.

class *Patch* σ π **where** *action* :: $\sigma \to \pi \to$ *Maybe* σ

Application of patches can also be reverted.

class (*Patch* σ π) $\Rightarrow$ *InvPatch* σ π **where** *undo* :: $\sigma \to \pi \to$ *Maybe* σ

This should be an inverse operation where defined:

data *PatchInvert* σ π = *PatchInvert*

instance (*InvPatch* σ π, *Eq* σ) $\Rightarrow$
$\qquad$ *Axiom* (*PatchInvert* σ π) ($\sigma \to \pi \to$ *Bool*) **where**
$\quad$ *axiomatic PatchInvert* = *Meta* ($\lambda s\ p \to$ **case** *action s p* **of**
$\qquad\qquad\qquad\qquad\qquad\qquad$ *Nothing* $\to$ *True*
$\qquad\qquad\qquad\qquad\qquad\qquad$ *Just s'* $\to$ *undo s' p* $\equiv$ *Just s*)

If the patch type has a *polarity*, that is some internal form of inversion, then the forward direction *action* suffices to imply the backward direction *undo*.

class *Polar* α **where**
$\quad$ *inv* :: $\alpha \to \alpha$

instance (*Patch* σ π, *Polar* π) $\Rightarrow$ *InvPatch* σ π **where**
$\quad$ *undo x p* = *action x* (*inv p*)

The most important forms of patch types are *group words*, made up from polarized primitives:

data *Polarity* = *Positive* | *Negative*

instance *Polar Polarity* **where**
$\quad$ *inv Positive* = *Negative*
$\quad$ *inv Negative* = *Positive*

data *Literal* α = *Literal Polarity* α

instance *Polar* (*Literal* α) **where**
$\quad$ *inv* (*Literal b x*) = *Literal* (*inv b*) *x*

instance (*InvPatch* σ α) $\Rightarrow$ *Patch* σ (*Literal* α) **where**
$\quad$ *action s* (*Literal Positive p*) = *action s p*
$\quad$ *action s* (*Literal Negative p*) = *undo s p*

Group words are essentially lists that polarize elementwise, but also reverse their order in the process, to accomodate for non-commutative groups.

newtype *Word* α = *Word* [*Literal* α]

instance *Polar* (*Word* α) **where**
$\quad$ *inv* (*Word w*) = *Word* (*reverse* (*map inv w*))

They act in the obvious way by folding, strictly over the *Maybe* monad.

instance (*InvPatch* σ α) $\Rightarrow$ *Patch* σ (*Word* α) **where**
$\quad$ *action s* (*Word w*) = *foldM action s w*

3.2   String Editing Operations

As an example instance of the generic theory, consider the editing of a character string. Suitable partial invertible atomic edit operations are:

- Inserting a given character at a given position if that does not exceed the end of the string, and inversely
- deleting a given character at a given position if it occurs there.

data *EditOp* = *Insert* | *Delete*

instance *Polar EditOp* **where**
   inv Insert = *Delete*
   inv Delete = *Insert*

data *Edit* = *Edit* { *op* :: *EditOp*, *pos* :: *Int*, *arg* :: *Char* }

instance *Polar Edit* **where**
   inv (*Edit f i x*) = *Edit* (*inv f*) *i x*

The operational semantics are modeled effectively by a type class that interprets the two operations, giving rise to an action on some state space.

class *Editable* α **where**
   insert :: $\alpha \to Int \to Char \to Maybe\ \alpha$
   delete :: $\alpha \to Int \to Char \to Maybe\ \alpha$

instance (*Editable* σ) $\Rightarrow$ *Patch* σ *Edit* **where**
   action s (*Edit Insert i x*) = *insert s i x*
   action s (*Edit Delete i x*) = *delete s i x*

The instance for the datatype *String* implements the above informal intuition.

instance *Editable String* **where**
   insert s   0 *x* = *return* (*x* : *s*)
   insert []   *i x* = *Nothing*
   insert (*y* : *t*) *i x* = *liftM* (*y*:) (*insert t* (*i* − 1) *x*)

   delete []   *i x* = *Nothing*
   delete (*y* : *t*) 0 *x* = *guard* (*x* ≡ *y*) ≫ *return t*
   delete (*y* : *t*) *i x* = *liftM* (*y*:) (*delete t* (*i* − 1) *x*)

3.3   Semantic Model

Group words only form a free monoid, in the obvious way inherited from the list type [], but partial applications of *flip action* induce a proper group of partial bijections on the state space. The extensional equality of induced group elements, and thus the *word problem* of the group presentation encoded in the action, is universally quantified, and thus hard to decide for large or even infinite state spaces. A heuristic evaluation would be sufficient as a meta-expression in simple offline checks, but not in negative positions, nor for online assertions, nor even in the operational layer of the codebase, such as in model animations.

This situation can be improved substantially by giving a semantic model in the form of an algebraic datatype with inductively derived equality, which is *fully abstract* in the sense that it admits a normal form where extensionally equal semantic functions are represented by the same data value.

For the example theory considered here, there is such a normal form of string-transducing automata. Because these automata do not require circular transitions, they can be modeled by a family of mutually linearly recursive datatypes, and evaluated by straightforward recursion.

$$
\begin{aligned}
\textbf{data } Editor &= Try\ Insertion \mid Fail \\
\textbf{data } Insertion &= Ins\ String\ Consumption \\
\textbf{data } Consumption &= Skip\ Insertion \\
&\mid Del\ Char\ Insertion \\
&\mid Return
\end{aligned}
$$

The operational idea is to apply each operator node to a position in an input string, advancing left to right. The detailed meaning of operators is as follows:

Fail. Applies to no string at all, immediately reject.
Try. Applies to some strings, begin processing at start position.
Ins. Insert zero or more characters before the position.
Skip. Advance the position over one character if available, otherwise reject.
Del. Remove the next character if available and matched, otherwise reject.
Return. Stop processing and accept, returning the remainder of the string as is.

The sorting of operators into different data types ensures that insertion and consumption alternate properly.

Note that, unlike random-access *Edit* terms, subsequent operator nodes are only ever applied to the original input string, not to the output of their predecessors. This is also the cause for the *Skip* and *Fail* operators which do not appear in the *Edit* language; they arise from attempting to delete a previously inserted character consistently and inconsistently, respectively.

The type *Insertion* is not to be constructed directly, but by the following smart constructor that avoids a degenerate corner case: Namely, insertions before and after a deletion are operationally indistinguishable. This ambiguity is avoided by avoiding insertions after a deletion, lumping adjacent insertions together beforehands, which preserves the desired normal form.

$$
\begin{aligned}
&ins :: String \rightarrow Consumption \rightarrow Insertion \\
&ins\ pre\ (Del\ y\ (Ins\ fix\ next)) = Ins\ (pre \mathbin{+\!\!+} fix)\ (Del\ y\ (Ins\ [\,]\ next)) \\
&ins\ prefix\ next \qquad\qquad\quad = Ins\ prefix\ next
\end{aligned}
$$

The semantic model type *Editor* covers the middle ground between the syntactic encoding *Word Edit* and the semantic state space *String*, in the sense that it instantiates both *Editable* and *Patch String*, giving the respective effective connections. The latter is the simpler one of the pair, and implements the intuition stated above.

```
instance Patch String Editor where
   action s Fail              = Nothing
   action s (Try steps)       = action s steps
instance Patch String Insertion where
   action s (Ins prefix next) = do t ← action s next
                                   return (prefix ++ t)

instance Patch String Consumption where
   action s Return            = return s
   action s (Skip   rest)     = do (x, t) ← uncons s
                                   u      ← action t rest
                                   return (x : u)
   action s (Del y rest)      = do (x, t) ← uncons s
                                   u      ← action t rest
                                   guard (x ≡ y)
                                   return u
```

The instantiation of *Editable* essentially amounts to splicing a single edit operation into an automaton while preserving the normal form. The technical details are too gruesome to be presented here in full.

```
instance Editable Editor ···
instance Editable Insertion ···
instance Editable Consumption ···
```

This instantiation implies an instance of *Patch Editor Edit*, which can be lifted to group words by folding over the *Maybe* monad.

```
semantics   :: Word Edit → Editor
semantics   = fromMaybe ∘ foldM action done ∘ toList

done :: Insertion
done = Ins [] Return

fromMaybe :: Maybe Insertion → Editor
fromMaybe = maybe Fail Try
```

The adequacy of the semantics can be stated concisely in terms of two propositions for soundness and full abstraction, respectively.

```
semantics_sound :: Meta (Word Edit → String → Bool)
semantics_sound = foreach (λx → patch_eq x (semantics x))

semantics_abstract :: Meta ((Editor, Editor) → Bool)
semantics_abstract = foreach (uncurry cons_eq)
```

The former uses extensional equivalence under *action* in positive position, hence the universal quantifiers can be nested, and sampled together at checking time.

```
patch_eq :: (Patch σ α, Patch σ β, Eq σ) ⇒ α → β → Meta (σ → Bool)
patch_eq x y = Meta (λs → action s x ≡ action s y)
```

By contrast, the latter conceptually uses extensional equivalence in negative position: "if two automata are extensionally equivalent then they are equal". This form of quantification cannot be approximated monotonically by sampling. Hence a constructive solution for the DeMorganized corresponding existential is required; if two automata are extensionally inequivalent, then a witness state for which they fail to coincide must be found.

$$cons\_eq :: (Eq\ \alpha,\ Witness\ (Diff\ \alpha)\ \beta) \Rightarrow \alpha \to \alpha \to Meta\ Bool$$
$$cons\_eq\ t\ u = Meta\ (t \equiv u \lor existsSome\ (t :\not\equiv u))$$

The operator $:\not\equiv$ of constructive logic is conveniently defined as the constructor of a new datatype *Diff*, since it requires an ad-hoc instance of *Witness* to hold each construction algorithm.

data $Diff\ \alpha = (:\not\equiv)\ \alpha\ \alpha$

It turns out that a straightforward algorithm requires three auxiliary constructive predicates, which bear witness that an automaton accepts some input, that an automaton rejects some input, and that one automaton accepts an input whereas another one rejects it, respectively.

data $Def\ \alpha \qquad = Def\ \alpha$
data $Undef\ \alpha \quad = Undef\ \alpha$
data $DefUndef\ \alpha = (:\geqslant)\ \alpha\ \alpha$

The implementations are too complex to be discussed here in detail.

instance $Witness\ (Diff \qquad Editor)\ String \cdots$
instance $Witness\ (Def \qquad Editor)\ String \cdots$
instance $Witness\ (Undef \qquad Editor)\ String \cdots$
instance $Witness\ (DefUndef\ Editor)\ String \cdots$

However, the intended semantics can be specified precisely, and checked, in a self-application of the meta-logical language.

$$def\_sound\_complete :: Meta\ (Editor \to Bool)$$
$$def\_sound\_complete = Meta$$
$$(\lambda x \to x \equiv Fail \lor exists\ (Def\ x)\ (\lambda s \to isJust\ (action\ s\ x)))$$
$$undef\_sound\_complete :: Meta\ (Editor \to Bool)$$
$$undef\_sound\_complete = Meta$$
$$(\lambda x \to isTotal\ x \lor exists\ (Undef\ x)\ (\lambda s \to \neg\ (isJust\ (action\ s\ x))))$$
$$def\_undef\_sound :: Meta\ ((Editor, Editor) \to Bool)$$
$$def\_undef\_sound = Meta$$
$$(\lambda(x, y) \to existsOrVacuous\ (x :\geqslant y)\ (\lambda s \to isJust\ (action\ s\ x) \land$$
$$\neg\ (isJust\ (action\ s\ y))))$$
$$diff\_sound\_complete :: Meta\ ((Editor, Editor) \to Bool)$$
$$diff\_sound\_complete = Meta$$
$$(\lambda(x, y) \to x \equiv y \lor exists\ (x :\not\equiv y)\ (\lambda s \to action\ s\ x \not\equiv action\ s\ y))$$

Note that the target *semantics_abstract* is a consequence of *diff_sound_complete* a fortiori already, but there is no obvious way to exploit that logical relationship in a checking framework.

Now we can operationalize the word problem by comparing automata,

$(\cong)$ :: *Word Edit* $\rightarrow$ *Word Edit* $\rightarrow$ *Bool*
$x \cong y = semantics\ x \equiv semantics\ y$

and conclude for instance that *fromList* [*Edit Insert* 2 'a', *Edit Delete* 3 'b']
$\cong$ *fromList* [*Edit Delete* 2 'b', *Edit Insert* 2 'a'].

3.4 Strategical Remarks

The above examples let us have a glimpse at the power of recursive tactics available in an embedded higher-order logical language: Equational reasoning about the data to be modeled is reduced to the word problem of a group presentation, an extensional property quantified over all possible inputs that can only be checked heuristically and positively. For broader checkability, this problem is factored through a normalizable automaton representation. The soundness and full abstraction of this semantics, and thus the equivalence of its equational reasoning, are checkable properties that contain existential quantification, for which constructive witnesses are given. The correctness and completeness of these constructions are universally quantified properties again, which can be checked heuristically.

Note that this does not mean we are going in circles; the correctness of the semantics needs only to be established once, and can be used as a shortcut for deciding equations of the original model henceforth. Yet the same language, tools and workflow are used for all phases.

4 Conclusion

We have proposed three advanced features of meta-logical language for offline checking of functional programs, namely meta-level marking, nominal axiomatics and constructive existentials. We have shown their implementation in the Haskell checking framework PureCheck, and demonstrated their use and interaction by means of a nontrivial executable modeling problem. Other aspects of PureCheck, such as ensuring the efficiency of deterministic sampling, are both work in progress and out of scope here, and shall be discussed in a forthcoming companion paper.

Dialectically, the stylistic ideal that underlies our experiments is contrary to the one employed in the construction of this paper: The checking paradigm expresses reasoning about the program in (a marked level of) the code, as opposed to the prose embellishment of the literate paradigm. We are hopeful that a thorough synthesis of the two can be demonstrated as synergetic and useful in the future.

Expressive offline checking language is an important step towards the reification of the algebraic concepts that pervade functional program design; consider the ubiquitous informal equational theory associated with Haskell type classes.

Marking the *Meta* level explicitly has not only the demonstrated advantages for the human reader, but may also serve as an anchor for meta-programming procedures, such as automatic test suite extraction without magic names.

The concept of constructive existentials is an explicitly controlled counterpart to implicit search strategies provided by the logical programming paradigm. Unlike SmartCheck, where constructive existentials are dismissed for often being hard to find in practice, we contend that in a (self-)educational context such as executable modeling, the understanding gained by implementing the construction witnesses for existential meta-logical properties of interest is rewarding rather than onerous. Furthermore we foresee interesting potential in the transfer of our ideas to a functional–logic language such as Curry [8] with built-in encapsulated search capabilities, but leave the exploration for future work.

References

1. Backus, J.: Can programming be liberated from the von Neumann style? A functional style and its Algebra of programs. Commun. ACM **21**(8), 613–641 (1978)
2. Chitil, O., Huch, F.: A pattern logic for prompt lazy assertions in Haskell. In: Horváth, Z., Zsók, V., Butterfield, A. (eds.) IFL 2006. LNCS, vol. 4449, pp. 126–144. Springer, Heidelberg (2007). https://doi.org/10.1007/978-3-540-74130-5_8
3. Claessen, K., Hughes, J.: QuickCheck: a lightweight tool for random testing of Haskell programs. SIGPLAN Notes **35**(9), 268–279 (2000). https://doi.org/10.1145/351240.351266
4. Clarke, L.A., Rosenblum, D.S.: A historical perspective on runtime assertion checking in software development. ACM SIGSOFT Softw. Eng. Notes **31**(3), 25–37 (2006). https://doi.org/10.1145/1127878.1127900
5. Cooper, J., Vik, J.O., Waltemath, D.: A call for virtual experiments: accelerating the scientific process. In: PeerJ PrePrints (2014). https://doi.org/10.7287/peerj.preprints.273v1
6. Coquand, T., Huet, G.: The calculus of constructions. Inf. Comput. **76**(2–3), 95–120 (1988). https://doi.org/10.1016/0890-5401(88)90005-3
7. George, F., Matt, B.: Property-based testing; a new approach to testing for assurance. Softw. Eng. Notes **22**(4), 74–80 (1997). https://doi.org/10.1145/263244.263267
8. Hanus, M.: Curry: a truly integrated functional logic language (2014). https://www-ps.informatik.uni-kiel.de/currywiki/
9. Norell, U.: Towards a practical programming language based on dependent type theory. Ph.D. thesis, Chalmers University of Technology (2007)
10. Jones, S.P.: Literate comments. The Haskell 98 report (2002). https://www.haskell.org/onlinereport/literate.html
11. Runciman, C., Naylor, M., Lindblad, F.: Smallcheck and lazy smallcheck: automatic exhaustive testing for small values. In: Haskell 2008: Proceedings of the First ACM SIGPLAN Symposium on Haskell, pp. 37–48 (2008). https://doi.org/10.1145/1411286.1411292

Implementation and Static Analysis

On the Performance of Bytecode Interpreters in Prolog

Philipp Körner(✉)(iD), David Schneider, and Michael Leuschel(iD)

Institut für Informatik, Heinrich Heine University Düsseldorf, Düsseldorf, Germany
{p.koerner,david.schneider,leuschel}@hhu.de

Abstract. The semantics and the recursive execution model of Prolog make it very natural to express language interpreters in form of AST (Abstract Syntax Tree) interpreters where the execution follows the tree representation of a program. An alternative implementation technique is that of bytecode interpreters. These interpreters transform the program into a compact and linear representation before evaluating it and are generally considered to be faster and to make better use of resources.

In this paper, we discuss different ways to express the control flow of interpreters in Prolog and present several implementations of AST and bytecode interpreters. On a simple language designed for this purpose, we evaluate whether techniques best known from imperative languages are applicable in Prolog and how well they perform. Our ultimate goal is to assess which interpreter design in Prolog is the most efficient as we intend to apply these results to a more complex language. However, we believe the analysis in this paper to be of more general interest.

1 Introduction

Writing simple language interpreters in Prolog is pretty straightforward. Definite clause grammars (DCGs) enable parsing of the program, and interpretation of the resulting abstract syntax tree (AST) can be expressed in an idiomatic, recursive way: Selecting which predicate to execute in order to evaluate a part of a program is done by unifying the part of the program to be executed next with the set of rules in Prolog's database that implement the language semantics. Subsequent execution steps can be chosen by using logic variables that are bound to substructures of the matched node.

Although this approach to interpreter construction is a natural match to Prolog, the question remains if it is the most efficient way to implement the instruction dispatching logic. In particular, we have developed such an interpreter [10] for the entire B language [1] and want to evaluate the potential for improving its performance, by using alternate implementation techniques.

Interpreters implemented in imperative languages, especially low-level languages, often make use of alternative techniques to implement the dispatching logic, taking advantage of available data structures and programming paradigms.

In this article, we explore if some of these techniques can be implemented in Prolog or applied in interaction with a Prolog runtime with the goal to assess

© Springer Nature Switzerland AG 2021
M. Hanus and C. Sacerdoti Coen (Eds.): WFLP 2020, LNCS 12560, pp. 41–56, 2021.
https://doi.org/10.1007/978-3-030-75333-7_3

```
# the initial environment (i.e. input): base = 2, exponent = 5

# the program
val = 1;
while exponent > 0 {
    val = val * base;
    exponent = exponent - 1;
}
```

Fig. 1. An ACOL program implementing a power function

whether the instruction dispatching for language interpreters can be made faster while keeping the language semantics in Prolog. In order to examine the performance of different dispatching models in Prolog, we have defined a simple imperative language named ACOL, which is briefly described in Sect. 2. For ACOL, we have created several implementations described in Sect. 3, that use different paradigms for the dispatching logic. In Sect. 4, we evaluate our approach on a set of benchmarks written in ACOL, executing the interpreters both on SICStus [3] and SWI-Prolog [15]. Finally, we give our conclusions in Sect. 5.

2   A Simple Language

As a means to evaluate different interpreter designs, we have defined a very simple and limited language named ACOL[1].

ACOL is an imperative language consisting of three kinds of statements: while-loops, if-then-else statements and variable assignments. The only supported value type is integer. Furthermore, ACOL offers a few arithmetic operators (addition, subtraction, multiplication and modulo), comparisons (less than (or equal to), greater than (or equal to) and equals), as well as a boolean **not** operator.

A simple ACOL program implementing a power function is shown in Fig. 1.

3   Interpreter Implementations

There are many ways to implement ACOL, in C as well as in Prolog. Considering several interpreter implementation techniques, in this section, we will describe possible designs of interpreters and the closely related representations of the ACOL programs in Prolog. The interpreters are based on either traversing the abstract syntax tree representation of a program or on compiling the program to bytecode [5] first and evaluating this more compact representation instead.

We opted to implement stack-based interpreters as their design tends to be simpler. The alternative – register-based virtual machines – are usually faster [13] and allow more advanced techniques such as register allocation optimisation in order to reduce the amount of load and store instructions. Yet, this endeavour would be far more involved and could be considered if this prototype already shows proper speed-ups.

---

[1] ACOL is *not* a backronym for ACOL is a computable language.

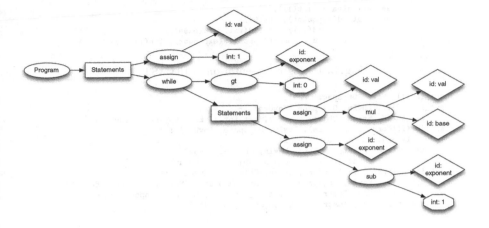

Fig. 2. AST

All interpreters share the same implementation of the language semantics exposed by an object-space API [11]. The objects space contains the code that creates integer objects, performs arithmetic operations, compares values, and manages the environment. In order to keep the implementations simple and compatible, all interpreters that we present call into this same object space. Nonetheless, the interpreters differ very much in the representation of the program and, hence, in the process of dispatching. The full code of all interpreters, benchmark scripts and results can be found at:

https://github.com/pkoerner/prolog-interpreters

In order to discuss the differences, we will translate the small example program shown in Fig. 1 into the different representations and show an excerpt of the interpretation logic for each paradigm. In Fig. 2, the AST for the example program is depicted.

3.1 AST Interpreter

The most idiomatic way to implement an interpreter in Prolog is in form of an AST interpreter since it synergises very well with its execution model.

The data structure used for this interpreter is the tree representation of the program as generated by the parser. In Prolog, the AST can be represented as a single term as shown in Fig. 3. The program itself is a Prolog list of statements. However, every statement is represented as its own sub-tree. Block statements, i.e. the body of `if` and `while` instructions, will contain a list of statements themselves.

```
[assign(id(val), int(1)),
 while(gt(id(exponent), int(0)),
        [assign(id(val), mul(id(val), id(base))),
         assign(id(exponent), sub(id(exponent), int(1)))])])]
```

Fig. 3. Prolog representation of the AST

```
ast_int([], Env, _Objspace, Env).
ast_int([H|T], EnvIn, Objspace, EnvOut) :-
    ast_int(H, EnvIn, Objspace, Env), ast_int(T, Env, Objspace, EnvOut).
ast_int(if(Cond, Then, Else), EnvIn, Objspace, EnvOut) :-
    eval(Cond, EnvIn, Objspace, X),
    (X == true -> ast_int(Then, EnvIn, Objspace, EnvOut)
        ; ast_int(Else, EnvIn, Objspace, EnvOut)).
ast_int(assign(id(Var), Expr), EnvIn, Objspace, EnvOut) :-
    eval(Expr, EnvIn, Objspace, Res), Objspace:store(EnvIn, Var, Res, EnvOut).
ast_int(while(Cond, Instr, _Invariant, _Variant), EnvIn, Objspace, EnvOut) :-
    ast_while(Cond, Instr, EnvIn, Objspace, EnvOut).
```

Fig. 4. Dispatching in a Prolog AST interpreter

The AST interpreter will examine the first element of the list, execute this statement and continue with the rest of the list, as can be seen in Fig. 4. Every sub-tree encountered this way is evaluated recursively.

Choosing the implementation for each node in the tree is done by unifying the current root node with the set of evaluation rules. This approach benefits from the first argument indexing [14] optimisation done by most Prolog systems.

3.2 Bytecode Interpreters

We have defined a simple set of bytecodes, described below, as a compilation target for ACOL programs. Based on these instructions we will introduce a series of bytecode interpreters that explore different implementation approaches in Prolog and C.

As many bytecode interpreters for other languages, ours are *stack-based*. Some opcodes may create or load objects and store them on the evaluation stack, e.g. push or load. Yet others may in turn consume objects from the stack and create a new one in return, e.g. add. Lastly, a single opcode is used to manipulate the environment, i.e. assign. An exhaustive list is shown in Table 1.

Imperative Bytecode Interpreter. Usually, bytecode interpreters are written in imperative languages, that are rather low-level, e.g. C, that allow more control about how objects are laid out in memory and provide fine-grained control over the flow of execution.

To introduce the concept of a bytecode interpreter, we present an implementation of ACOL beyond Prolog, that is purely written in C.

Table 1. A bytecode for the described language

#	Name	Arguments	Semantics
10	jump	4 bytes encoded PC	Jumps to new PC
11	jump-if-false	4 bytes encoded PC	Jumps to new PC if top element is falsey
12	jump-if-true	4 bytes encoded PC	Jumps to new PC if top element is truthy
20	push1	1 byte encoded integer	Push the argument on the stack
21	push4	4 bytes encoded integer	Push the argument on the stack
40	load	4 bytes encoded variable ID	Push variable on the stack
45	assign	4 bytes encoded variable ID	Store top of the stack in variable
197	mod	–	Pop operands, push result of operation
198	mul	–	Pop operands, push result of operation
199	sub	–	Pop operands, push result of operation
200	add	–	Pop operands, push result of operation
240	not	–	Pop operand, push negation
251	eq	–	Pop operands, push result of comparison
252	le	–	Pop operands, push result of comparison
253	lt	–	Pop operands, push result of comparison
254	ge	–	Pop operands, push result of comparison
255	gt	–	Pop operands, push result of comparison

The bytecode is stored as a block of memory, that can be interpreted as an array of bytes. The index of this array that should be interpreted next is called the program counter. After that opcode is executed, the program counter is incremented by one, plus the size of its arguments. However, it may be set to an arbitrary index by opcodes implementing jumps. Integer arguments are encoded in reverse byte order.

The dispatching logic is implemented as a `switch`-statement that is contained in a loop. An excerpt of the implementation of our bytecode interpreter in C is shown in Fig. 5. Every `case` block contains an implementation of that specific opcode. After the opcode is executed, the program counter is advanced or reset and the next iteration of the main loop is commenced.

C-Interfaces. We made the digression into an interpreter written in C not only to present the concept of bytecode interpreters. Instead, we can utilise the same dispatching logic, but instead of calling an object space that is implemented in C, we can use the C interfaces provided by the Prolog runtimes we consider (SICStus and SWI-Prolog) to call arbitrary Prolog predicates. This way, we can query the aforementioned object space that contains the semantics of ACOL, but is implemented in Prolog. An excerpt when using the C interface of SWI-Prolog is shown in Fig. 6.

For the C-interface, we re-use the linear bytecode from the Prolog interpreter above. The list of bytecodes is passed to C, which allocates a C array, iterates over the list and copies the instructions into the array. Then, the main loop dispatches in C, but the objects on the evaluation stack are created and the operations are executed by Prolog predicates.

```
while (pc < bc_len) {
    unsigned char *arg = bc + pc + 1;
    switch (bc[pc]) {
        case JUMP:
            pc = decode_arg4(arg); break;
        case LOAD:
            index = decode_arg4(arg);
            push(stack, env[index]);
            pc += 5; break;
        case ASSIGN:
            env[arg] = pop(stack);
            pc += 5; break;
        case ADD:
            b = pop(stack);
            a = pop(stack);
            push(stack, add(a, b));
            pc++; break;
        // ... many further cases
    }
}
```

Fig. 5. Dispatching logic in C

```
while (pc < bc_len) {
    unsigned char *arg = bc + pc + 1;
    switch (bc[pc]) {
        case JUMP:
            pc = decode_arg4(arg); break;
        case LOAD:
            index = decode_arg4(arg);
            push(stack, env[index]);
            pc += 5; break;
        case ASSIGN:
            index = decode_arg4(arg);
            PL_put_term(env[index], pop(s));
            pc += 5; break;
        case ADD:
            arg1 = PL_new_term_refs(3);
            arg2 = arg1 + 1;
            var = arg1 + 2;
            PL_put_term(arg2, pop(s));
            PL_put_term(arg1, pop(s));
            PL_call_predicate(NULL,
                              PL_Q_NORMAL,
                              predicate_add,
                              arg1);
            push(s, var);
            pc++; break;
        // ... many further cases
    }
}
```

Fig. 6. Dispatching logic using SWI-Prolog's C-Interface

Prolog Facts. The main issue with bytecode interpreters in Prolog is the efficient implementation of jumps to other parts of the bytecode. With an interpreter in C, all we have to do is to re-assign the program counter variable. Prolog, however, does not offer arrays with constant-time indexing[2].

The idiomatic way to simulate an array would be to use a Prolog list, but on this data structure we can perform lookups only in $\mathcal{O}(n)$. Yet, there are other representations of the program that allow jumping to another position faster.

One way to express such a lookup in $\mathcal{O}(1)$ is to transform the bytecode into Prolog terms bytecode(ProgramCounter, Instruction, Arguments). Those terms are written into a separate Prolog module that is loaded afterwards. The first argument indexing optimisation then allows lookups in constant time.

In contrast to an interpreter written in C, it does not perform well to encode integer arguments into reverse byte-order arguments. Instead, we use the Prolog primitives, i.e. integers for values and atoms for variable identifiers.

Figure 7 shows a module that is generated from the bytecode. The interpreter fetches the instruction located at the current program counter, executes it and increments the program counter accordingly. This is repeated until it encounters a special zero instruction denoting the end of the bytecode – here at location 54.

---

[2] While, again, interoperability with C allows embedding of such data structures, standard library predicates usually only offer logarithmic access.

```
bytecode(0, 20, 1).           % push integer 1 on the stack
bytecode(2, 45, val).         % pop value from stack, store in val
bytecode(7, 40, exponent).    % push value of exponent
bytecode(12, 20, 0).          % push constant 0
bytecode(14, 255, []).        % greater-than comparison
bytecode(15, 11, 54).         % jump-if-false to location 55 (exit loop)
bytecode(20, 40, val).        % push value of val
bytecode(25, 40, base).       % push value of base
bytecode(30, 198, []).        % multiplication of arguments on the stack
bytecode(31, 45, val).        % store result in val
bytecode(36, 40, exponent).   % load exponent
bytecode(41, 20, 1).          % push constant 1
bytecode(43, 199, []).        % subtract arguments on stack
bytecode(44, 45, exponent).   % store result in exponent
bytecode(49, 10, 7).          % jump to beginning of loop
bytecode(54, 0, []).          % terminate instruction
```

Fig. 7. Bytecode as Prolog facts

```
fact_int(PC, Objspace, Env, Stack, REnv) :-
    generated:bc(PC, Instr, Args), % fetch the instruction
    fact_int(Instr, Args, PC, Stack, Env, Objspace, REnv).
fact_int(200, _Args, PC, [Y, X|Stack], Env, Objspace, REnv) :-
    Objspace:add(X, Y, Res), NewPC is PC + 1,
    fact_int(NewPC, Objspace, Env, [Res|Stack], REnv).
% fact_int also has implementations of all the other bytecodes...
```

Fig. 8. Dispatching in the facts-based interpreter

The dispatching mechanism is shown in Fig. 8. Similar to an interpreter in C, every opcode has an implementation in Prolog that calls into the object space. Any rule of fact_int is equivalent to a case statement in C.

Sub-Bytecodes. Another design is based on the idea that a program is executed *block-wise*, i.e. a series of instructions that is guaranteed to be executed in this specific order. This is very simple since ACOL does not include a goto-statement that allows arbitrary jumps. From a programmer's point of view, blocks are the bodies of while-loops or those of if-then-else statements.

Instead of linearising the entire bytecode, only a block is linearised at once. In order to deal with blocks that are contained by another block (e.g. nested loops), two special opcodes are added. They are used to suspend the execution of the current block and look up the *sub-bytecodes* of the contained blocks that are referenced via its arguments. After those sub-bytecodes are executed, the execution of the previous bytecode is resumed.

The special if-opcode references the blocks of the corresponding then- and else- branches. After the condition is evaluated, only the required block is looked up and executed. The other special opcode for while-loops references the bytecode of the condition that is expected to leave true or false on the stack,

```
[20, 1, 45, val, % val = 1
 2, 0, 1]       % while (condition encoded in sub-bytecode 0,
                %         body encoded in sub-bytecode 1)

% Sub-bytecodes
sbc(0, [40, exponent, 20, 0, 255]).
sbc(1, [40, val, 40, base, 198, 45, val, 40, exponent, 20, 1, 199]).
```

Fig. 9. Bytecode with sub-bytecodes

```
bc_int([], Env, Stack, _Objspace, Env, Stack).
bc_int([H|R], Env, Stack, Objspace, REnv, RStack) :-
    bc_int2(H,R, Env, Stack, Objspace, REnv, RStack).
% special bytecodes for evaluating blocks of an if-statement
bc_int2(1, [T, E|R], Env, [Cond|Stack], Objspace, REnv, RStack) :-
    (Cond == true -> subbytecodes:sbc(T, Then),
                     h_bc_int(Then, [], Env, Objspace, TEnv)
     ;  subbytecodes:sbc(E, Else),
                     h_bc_int(Else, [], Env, Objspace, TEnv)),!,
    bc_int(R, TEnv, Stack, Objspace, REnv, RStack).
% special bytecodes for evaluating blocks of a while-loop
bc_int2(2, [C, I|R], Env, Stack, Objspace, REnv, RStack) :-
    subbytecodes:sbc(C, Cond),
    bc_int(Cond, Env, [], Objspace, Env, [Res]),
    (Res == true -> subbytecodes:sbc(I, Instr),
                    h_bc_int(Instr, [], Env, Objspace, T),!,
                    bc_int2(2, [C, I|R], T, Stack, Objspace, REnv, RStack)
     ; !, bc_int(R, Env, Stack, Objspace, REnv, RStack)).

bc_int2(200, R, Env, [Y, X|Stack], Objspace, REnv, RStack) :-
    Objspace:add(X, Y, Res),!,
    bc_int(R, Env, [Res|Stack], Objspace, REnv, RStack).
% bc_int2 also has implementations of all the other bytecodes...
```

Fig. 10. Dispatching on bytecodes with sub-bytecodes

as well as the body of the loop. The blocks corresponding to condition and body are evaluated in turn until the condition does not hold any more, so the execution of its parent block can continue. Similar to the facts in the interpreter above, the sub-bytecodes are asserted into their own module to allow fast lookups.

Figure 9 shows an example that includes the special opcode for the while-statement, and Fig. 10 shows an excerpt of the dispatching logic used for this interpreter. The recursion in bc_int2 will update the bytecode list with its tail instead of manipulating a program counter. Hence, in this implementation, the interpreter can only move forward inside of a block. If it is required to move backwards in the program, it is only possible to re-start at the beginning of a block.

```
assign(id(val), int(1),
  while(gt(id(exponent), int(0)),
    assign(id(val), mul(id(val), id(base)),
      assign(id(exponent), sub(id(exponent), int(1)),
        while(gt(id(exponent), int(0)),
          ...)))
end))
```

Fig. 11. Rational tree representation

3.3   Rational Trees

Based on [4], we have created implementations of an AST and a bytecode interpreter for ACOL that use the idea of rational trees to represent the program being
evaluated. This technique aims to improve the performance of jumps by using
recursive data structures containing references to the following instructions.

AST Interpreter with Rational Trees. Since ACOL does not include a
concept of arbitrary jumps as used in [4], it is not possible to achieve the speed-
up described in the referenced paper. However, we can make use of the basic idea
for the representation of programs: every statement has a pointer to its successor
statement.

In our naive AST interpreter, a new Prolog stack frame is used for every level
of nested loops and if-statements. Instead of returning from each evaluation to
the predicate that dispatched to the sub-statement, we can make use of Prolog's
tail-recursion optimisation and continue with the next statements directly.

For our example program, we generate an infinite data structure for the
while-loop depicted in Fig. 11. The concept of rational trees allows us to have
the while-term re-appearing in its own body, so it has not to be saved in a stack
frame.

The last statement end is artificially added to indicate the end of the program
so that the interpreter may halt.

Then, the dispatching logic is still very similar to the naive AST interpreter
as shown in Fig. 12.

Bytecode-Interpreter with Rational Trees. In Prolog, rational trees can
also be used for bytecodes. Jumps are removed from that representation entirely.
While-loops are unrolled into an infinite amount of alternated bytecodes of the
condition and if-statements that contain the body of the loop in their then-
branch and the next statement after the loop in their else-branch. An example
is shown in Fig. 13.

At first glance, it looks weird that the opcode integers are replaced by human-
readable descriptions. However, functors are limited to atoms and, then, there is
not much difference between atoms that contain only a number or short readable
names. We chose the latter one because they are by far more comprehensible.

The dispatching is pretty similar to the AST interpreter that utilises rational
trees, as shown in Fig. 14. The main difference between those two interpreters

```
rt_int(end, Env, _, Env) :- !.
rt_int(assign(id(Var), Expr, Next), Env, Objspace, REnv) :-
    eval(Expr, Env, Objspace, Res),
    Objspace:store(Env, Var, Res, EnvOut), !,
    rt_int(Next, EnvOut, Objspace, REnv).
rt_int(if(Cond, Then, Else), Env, Objspace, REnv) :-
    eval(Cond, Env, Objspace, V),
    (V == true -> !, rt_int(Then, Env, Objspace, REnv)
                ; !, rt_int(Else, Env, Objspace, REnv)).
rt_int(while(Cond, Instrs, Else), Env, Objspace, REnv) :-
    eval(Cond, Env, Objspace, V),
    (V == true -> !, rt_int(Instrs, Env, Objspace, REnv)
                ; !, rt_int(Else, Env, Objspace, REnv)).
```

Fig. 12. Dispatching in a rational tree interpreter

```
push(1, assign(val,                              % code before the loop
  load(exponent, push(0, gt(                     % condition (1)
    if(load(val, load(base, mul(store(val,       % while-body (1)
      load(exponent, push(1, sub(store(exponent, % while-body (1)
        load(exponent, push(0, gt(               % condition (2)
          if(load(val, load(base(, ....))),      % while-body (2)
            end)))))))))))                       % end of while (2)
      end))))))                                   % end of while (1)
```

Fig. 13. Bytecode with rational trees

is that this one uses a simulated stack to evaluate terms instead of Prolog's call stack.

4 Evaluation

To compare the performance of the different interpreters for ACOL, we selected a set of different benchmarks. Because the language is very limited, it is hard to design "real-world programs". Yet, execution of any arbitrary program will give insight of the performance of the dispatching logic.

In this section, we present those benchmarks and compare their results. Each program was executed with every interpreter ten times. The runtime consists only of the time spent in the interpreter. Compilation time is excluded, as it is not implemented efficiently and, ultimately, not relevant.

The benchmarks were run on a machine that runs a Linux with a 4.15.0-108-generic 64-bit kernel on an Intel i7-7700HQ CPU @ 2.80 GHz. No benchmarks ran in parallel. Two Prolog implementations were considered: SICStus Prolog 4.6.0, a commercial product, and SWI-Prolog 8.2.1, a free open-source implementation. All C code was compiled by gcc 7.5.0 with the -O3-flag.

Since ACOL does not offer complex features, we expect that the dispatching claims a bigger share of the runtime than the actual operations.

```
rt_bc_int(end, Env, Stack, _Objspace, Env, Stack).
rt_bc_int(if(Then, Else), Env, [X|Stack], Objspace, REnv, RStack) :-
    (X == true -> !, rt_bc_int(Then, Env, Stack, Objspace, REnv, RStack)
        ; !, rt_bc_int(Else, Env, Stack, Objspace, REnv, RStack)).
rt_bc_int(push(Arg, Next), Env, Stack, Objspace, REnv, RStack) :-
    Objspace:create_integer(Arg, Val),!,
    rt_bc_int(Next, Env, [Val|Stack], Objspace, REnv, RStack).
rt_bc_int(load(Arg, Next), Env, Stack, Objspace, REnv, RStack) :-
    Objspace:lookup(Arg, Env, Val), !,
    rt_bc_int(Next, Env, [Val|Stack], Objspace, REnv, RStack).
rt_bc_int(add(Next), Env, [Y, X|Stack], Objspace, REnv, RStack) :-
    Objspace:add(X, Y, Res), !,
    rt_bc_int(Next, Env, [Res|Stack], Objspace, REnv, RStack).
% rt_bc_int implements all other opcodes as well...
```

Fig. 14. Dispatching in a bytecode interpreter with rational trees

```
while (start < V) {
    if (V mod start == 0) {
        is_prime := 0;
    } else {
        is_prime := is_prime;
    }
    start := start + 1;
}
```

Fig. 15. Prime tester program

```
i := 1;                     i := 1;
while i < n {               while i < n {
    b := b + a;                 b := b + a mod 1000000;
    a := b - a;                 a := b - a mod 1000000;
    i := i + 1;                 i := i + 1;
}                           }
```

Fig. 16. Fibonacci programs

4.1 Benchmarks

Prime Tester. The first benchmark is a naive prime tester. The program is depicted in Fig. 15. The environment was pre-initialised with is_prime := 1, start := 2 , and V := 34 265 341.

Fibonacci. Another benchmark is the calculation of the Fibonacci sequence (see Fig. 16). However, we expect that most of the execution time will consist of the addition and subtraction of two large numbers and that the interpreter overhead itself is rather small. Therefore, a second version that calculates the sequence modulo 1 000 000 is included.

Again, the environment is pre-initialised, in this case with a := 0, b := 1 and n := 400 000. To ensure a significant runtime for the second version, the input is modified so it calculates a longer sequence, i.e. n := 10 000 000.

Generated ASTs. Lastly, some programs were generated pseudo-randomly. Such a generated AST consists of 20 to 50 statements that are uniformly chosen from while-loops, if-statements and assignments. The body of a loop and both

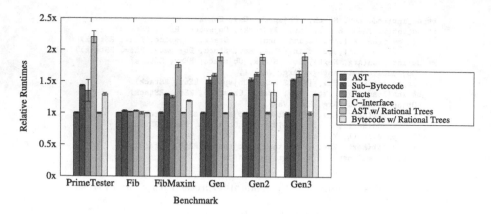

Fig. 17. Relative runtimes in SICStus, normalised to the runtime of the AST interpreter

branches of if-statements also consist of 20 to 50 statements. However, if the nesting exceeds a certain depth, only assignments are generated for this block.

In order to guarantee termination, while-loops are always executed 20 times. An assignment is artificially inserted before the loop that resets a loop counter, as well as another assignment that increments this variable at the beginning of the loop.

For assignments and if-conditions, a small subtree is generated. The generator chooses uniformly between five predetermined identifiers, constants ranging from −1 to 3, as well as additions and subtractions. If-conditions have to include exactly one comparison operator.

The generator does include neither multiplications, because they caused very large integers that slowed down the Prolog execution time significantly, nor modulo operations, to avoid division by zero errors.

Three different benchmarks were generated using arbitrary seeds. Their purpose is to complement the other three handwritten benchmarks, which are rather small and might benefit from caching of the entire AST.

4.2 Results

The results of the benchmarks are shown in Table 2. The lines labelled "AST" refer to the implementation of the naive AST interpreter presented in Sect. 3.1, the ones with "Sub-Bytecodes", "Facts" and "C-Interface" refer to the corresponding bytecode interpreters discussed in Sect. 3.2. Finally, "AST" and "BC w/Rational Trees" are the AST and bytecode interpreters based on rational trees presented in Sect. 3.3. The mean value is determined by the geometric mean as proposed by [8]. Though not listed, the interpreter purely written in C is 2–3 orders of magnitudes faster[3] and executes each benchmark in less than a second.

---

[3] A fair comparison is not possible since the C interpreter does not support unbounded integer values.

Table 2. Mean runtimes in seconds including the 0.95 confidence interval. The value in parentheses describes the normalised runtime (on the basis of the AST interpreter). The fastest runtimes per benchmark and interpreter are highlighted.

Benchmark	Interpreter	SICStus	SWI-Prolog
	AST	54.53 ± 0.49 (1.00)	242.84 ± 3.96 (1.00)
	Sub-Bytecodes	78.03 ± 0.59 (1.43)	316.44 ± 1.89 (1.30)
Prime Tester	Facts	73.50 ± 9.39 (1.35)	330.89 ± 2.51 (1.36)
	C-Interface	119.94 ± 5.13 (2.20)	54.83 ± 0.98 (0.23)
	AST w/ Rational Trees	54.26 ± 0.57 (1.00)	229.65 ± 2.28 (0.95)
	BC w/ Rational Trees	70.65 ± 1.19 (1.30)	261.39 ± 5.58 (1.08)
	AST	9.86 ± 0.05 (1.00)	5.54 ± 0.09 (1.00)
	Sub-Bytecodes	10.16 ± 0.13 (1.03)	6.36 ± 0.15 (1.15)
Fibonacci	Facts	10.00 ± 0.07 (1.01)	6.49 ± 0.09 (1.17)
	C-Interface	10.16 ± 0.09 (1.03)	2.58 ± 0.06 (0.47)
	AST w/ Rational Trees	9.84 ± 0.19 (1.00)	5.39 ± 0.09 (0.97)
	BC w/ Rational Trees	9.83 ± 0.06 (1.00)	5.63 ± 0.10 (1.02)
	AST	24.03 ± 0.30 (1.00)	96.90 ± 1.72 (1.00)
	Sub-Bytecodes	31.03 ± 0.26 (1.29)	122.86 ± 1.54 (1.27)
Fibonacci (Maxint)	Facts	30.13 ± 0.48 (1.25)	131.38 ± 3.68 (1.36)
	C-Interface	42.23 ± 0.90 (1.76)	22.65 ± 0.48 (0.23)
	AST w/ Rational Trees	24.05 ± 0.17 (1.00)	94.36 ± 1.15 (0.97)
	BC w/ Rational Trees	28.63 ± 0.25 (1.19)	103.93 ± 0.70 (1.07)
	AST	12.96 ± 0.16 (1.00)	60.64 ± 0.59 (1.00)
	Sub-Bytecodes	19.71 ± 0.70 (1.52)	69.26 ± 0.49 (1.14)
Generated	Facts	20.76 ± 0.33 (1.60)	73.89 ± 0.45 (1.22)
	C-Interface	24.49 ± 0.82 (1.89)	10.30 ± 0.18 (0.17)
	AST w/ Rational Trees	12.89 ± 0.14 (0.99)	58.35 ± 1.45 (0.96)
	BC w/ Rational Trees	16.90 ± 0.20 (1.30)	61.98 ± 1.16 (1.02)
	AST	19.01 ± 0.18 (1.00)	83.18 ± 0.80 (1.00)
	Sub-Bytecodes	29.11 ± 0.48 (1.53)	102.17 ± 1.48 (1.23)
Generated2	Facts	30.78 ± 0.55 (1.62)	109.08 ± 2.35 (1.31)
	C-Interface	35.89 ± 0.92 (1.89)	15.07 ± 0.24 (0.18)
	AST w/ Rational Trees	19.10 ± 0.26 (1.00)	81.05 ± 0.39 (0.97)
	BC w/ Rational Trees	25.28 ± 2.96 (1.33)	90.44 ± 1.21 (1.09)
	AST	12.37 ± 0.22 (1.00)	55.52 ± 1.34 (1.00)
	Sub-Bytecodes	18.93 ± 0.20 (1.53)	66.00 ± 0.76 (1.19)
Generated3	Facts	20.06 ± 0.64 (1.62)	70.49 ± 0.45 (1.27)
	C-Interface	23.51 ± 0.71 (1.90)	9.79 ± 0.22 (0.18)
	AST w/ Rational Trees	12.38 ± 0.30 (1.00)	52.96 ± 1.12 (0.95)
	BC w/ Rational Trees	16.10 ± 0.11 (1.30)	60.07 ± 0.97 (1.08)

Figure 17 shows the results specific for SICStus Prolog. There is no discernible performance difference between the naive AST interpreter and the ones utilising rational trees. Independent of the benchmark, the bytecode interpreters based on sub-bytecodes and on Prolog facts are slow in comparison. One can observe a performance loss of about 25–35 % for the small handwritten programs, where we would expect caching effects to be the largest, and around 50–60% for the larger, generated programs. With our initial version of the interpreter dispatching in C,

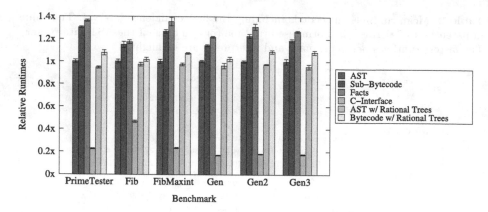

Fig. 18. Relative runtimes in SWI-Prolog, normalised to the runtime of the AST interpreter

we reported an issue that was related with SICStus' FLI garbage collector. Now, it usually requires twice as much time to execute the benchmarks compared to the AST-based interpreters.

The results utilising SWI-Prolog are shown in Fig. 18. Overall, they paint a similar picture to the results for SICStus. However, the dispatching using SWI-Prolog's C-interface is very fast – compared to the AST interpreter, it can achieve more than a 5× speed-up.

As an aside, one can clearly see that SICStus Prolog, as a commercial product, outperforms SWI-Prolog, an open-source implementation, on most benchmarks. This might be caused by the JIT SICStus Prolog utilises, though there are no public information available. Yet, the gap between SWI-Prolog and SICStus closes: compared to our initial experiments in 2015, SWI-Prolog is about twice as fast today.

5   Conclusions, Related and Future Work

In this paper, we presented the language ACOL and multiple ways to implement it as AST as well as bytecode interpreters. We designed several benchmarks in order to evaluate their performance using different implementations of Prolog.

Our results suggest that if an interpreter is to be implemented in Prolog, the implementation as an AST interpreter already is very performant. It is simply not worth the hassle of writing and maintaining a bytecode compiler. Furthermore, an AST interpreter does not involve any additional compilation overhead as it can directly work on the data structure returned by the parser.

However, SWI-Prolog's C interface performs very well. Surprisingly, even on the Fibonacci example with unlimited integers, where addition of unlimited integers is rather time-consuming, it beats the run-time of the AST interpreter by a factor of two. Additional work is required to determine whether these findings are applicable for more complex languages, that would also facilitate the creation of more sensible benchmarks.

Investigations stemming from other interpreted programming languages suggest that register-based execution models might yield additional speed-up [6,7,13]. While we do not expect a speed-up of around an order of magnitude that we initially hoped for, this might be a worthwhile research direction in order to gain more optimal performance, especially regarding the large body of research of further optimisation.

Rossi and Sivalingam explored dispatching techniques in C based bytecode interpreters [12], with the result that a less portable approach of composing the code in memory before executing it yielded the best results. The techniques discussed in that article could be used in combination with SWI-Prolog to further improve the instruction dispatching performance in C.

An alternative for improving the execution time of a program, that was not discussed here, is partial evaluation [9]. We intend to investigate the impact of offline partial evaluation when compiling a subset of the described interpreters for our benchmarks.

In the future, it would also be interesting to evaluate the effects of different interpreter designs in other Prolog dialects, especially those that are not based on the WAM [2,14]. Examples include Ciao (WAM-based with powerful analysis), BinProlog (specialised version of the WAM) and Mercury (functional influences with many optimisations).

References

1. Abrial, J.-R.: The B-Book. Cambridge University Press, Cambridge (1996)
2. Aït-Kaci, H.: Warren's abstract machine - a tutorial reconstruction (1991)
3. Carlsson, M., Mildner, P.: SICStus Prolog - the first 25 years. Theory Pract. Log. Program. **12**(1–2), 35–66 (2012)
4. Carro, M.: An application of rational trees in a logic programming interpreter for a procedural language. CoRR, cs.DS/0403028, March 2004
5. Dahm, M.: Byte code engineering. In: Cap, C.H. (ed.) JIT 1999. INFORMAT, pp. 267–277. Springer, Heidelberg (1999). https://doi.org/10.1007/978-3-642-60247-4_25
6. Davis, B., Beatty, A., Casey, K., Gregg, D., Waldron, J.: The case for virtual register machines. In: Proceedings IVME, pp. 41–49. ACM (2003)
7. Fang, R., Liu, S.: A performance survey on stack-based and register-based virtual machines. arXiv preprint arXiv:1611.00467 (2016)
8. Fleming, P.J., Wallace, J.J.: How not to lie with statistics: the correct way to summarize benchmark results. Commun. ACM **29**(3), 218–221 (1986)
9. Jones, N.D., Gomard, C.K., Sestoft, P.: Partial Evaluation and Automatic Program Generation. Prentice Hall, Hoboken (1993)
10. Leuschel, M., Butler, M.J.: ProB: an automated analysis toolset for the B method. STTT **10**(2), 185–203 (2008)
11. The PyPy Project. The Object Space (2015). http://pypy.readthedocs.org/en/latest/objspace.html. Accessed 12 Aug 2020
12. Rossi, M., Sivalingam, K.: A survey of instruction dispatch techniques for byte-code interpreters. In: Seminar on Mobile Code (1996)

13. Shi, Y., Casey, K., Ertl, M.A., Gregg, D.: Virtual machine showdown: stack versus registers. Trans. Archit. Code Optim. 4(4), 1–36 (2008)
14. Warren, D.H.D.: An abstract Prolog instruction set. Technical report 309, Artificial Intelligence Center - SRI International, Stanford (1983)
15. Wielemaker, J., Schrijvers, T., Triska, M., Lager, T.: SWI-Prolog. Theory Pract. Log. Program. 12(1–2), 67–96 (2012)

Memoized Pull-Tabbing for Functional Logic Programming

Michael Hanus$^{(\boxtimes)}$ and Finn Teegen

Institut für Informatik, CAU Kiel, 24098 Kiel, Germany
{mh,fte}@informatik.uni-kiel.de

Abstract. Pull-tabbing is an evaluation technique for functional logic programs which computes all non-deterministic results in a single graph structure. Pull-tab steps are local graph transformations to move non-deterministic choices towards the root of an expression. Pull-tabbing is independent of a search strategy so that different strategies (depth-first, breadth-first, parallel) can be used to extract the results of a computation. It has been used to compile functional logic languages into imperative or purely functional target languages. Pull-tab steps might duplicate choices in case of shared subexpressions. This could result in a dramatic increase of execution time compared to a backtracking implementation. In this paper we propose a refinement which avoids this efficiency problem while keeping all the good properties of pull-tabbing. We evaluate a first implementation of this improved technique in the Julia programming language.

1 Introduction

Functional logic languages [7] combine the main features of functional and logic languages in a single programming model. In particular, demand-driven evaluation of expressions is amalgamated with non-deterministic search for values. This is the basis of optimal evaluation strategies [4] and yields a tight integration between specifications and code [8]. However, it also demands for advanced implementation techniques—an active research area in declarative programming. This paper proposes a new implementation model which combines advantages of existing models in a novel way.

The main challenge in the implementation of functional logic languages is the handling of non-determinism. For instance, consider the following operations (in example programs we use Curry syntax [21] which is close to Haskell):

```
flip 0 = 1          coin = 0
flip 1 = 0          coin = 1
```

`flip` is a conventional function whereas `coin` is a *non-deterministic operation* [17], an important concept of contemporary functional logic languages. A non-deterministic operation might yield more than one result on the same input, e.g., `coin` has values 0 and 1 (see [7,17] for discussions of this concept). Due to the

© Springer Nature Switzerland AG 2021
M. Hanus and C. Sacerdoti Coen (Eds.): WFLP 2020, LNCS 12560, pp. 57–73, 2021.
https://doi.org/10.1007/978-3-030-75333-7_4

importance of non-deterministic operations, Curry defines an archetypal *choice* operation "?" by

```
x ? _ = x
_ ? y = y
```

so that one can define `coin` also by "`coin = 0 ? 1`". In functional logic languages, non-deterministic operations can be used as any other operation, in particular, as arguments to other (deterministic) operations, e.g., as in "`flip coin`". It is important to keep in mind that any evaluation of an expression might lead to a non-deterministic choice. We review some existing approaches to deal with such choices during program execution.

Backtracking implements a choice by selecting one alternative to proceed the computation. If a computation comes to an end (failure or success), the state before the choice is restored and the next alternative is taken. Backtracking is the traditional approach of Prolog systems so that it is used in implementations that compile functional logic languages into Prolog, like PAKCS [5,19] or TOY [25]. The major disadvantage of backtracking is its operational incompleteness: if the first alternative does not terminate, no result will be computed.

Copying or *cloning* avoids this disadvantage by copying the context of a choice and proceed with both alternatives in parallel or by interleaving steps. Due to the cost of copying when a choice occurs deeply in an expression, it has been used only in experimental implementations, e.g., [10].

Pull-tabbing is another approach to avoid the incompleteness of backtracking by keeping all alternatives in one computation structure, typically, a graph. It was first sketched in [2] and formally explored in [3]. In contrast to copying, a pull-tab step is a local transformation which moves a choice occurring in an argument of an operation outside this operation. For instance,

```
flip (0 ? 1)   →   (flip 0) ? (flip 1)
```

is a pull-tab step. Pull-tabbing is used in implementations targeting complete search strategies, e.g., KiCS [15], KiCS2 [13], or Sprite [11]. Although pull-tab steps have local effects only, iterated pull-tab steps move choices to the root of an expression. If expressions with choices are shared (e.g., by `let` expressions or multiple occurrences of argument variables in rule bodies), pull-tab steps might produce multiple copies of the same choice. This could lead to unsoundness, which can be fixed by attaching identifiers to choices [3], and to duplication of computations. The latter is a serious problem of pull-tabbing implementations [18]. In this paper, we propose a working solution to this problem by adding a kind of memoization to pull-tabbing. With this extension, pull-tabbing becomes faster than backtracking and at the same time flexible and operationally complete search strategies can be used.

This paper is structured as follows. After reviewing some details of functional logic programming and the pull-tab strategy along with its performance issues in the following two sections, we present our solution to these problems in Sect. 4. A prototypical implementation of our improved strategy is sketched in Sect. 5 and evaluated by some benchmarks in Sect. 6. Related work is discussed in Sect. 7 before we conclude.

2   Functional Logic Programming with Curry

The declarative multi-paradigm language Curry [21], considered in this paper for concrete examples, combines features from functional programming (demand-driven evaluation, parametric polymorphism, higher-order functions) and logic programming (computing with partial information, unification, constraints). The syntax of Curry is close to Haskell[1] [27]. In addition, Curry allows free (logic) variables in conditions and right-hand sides of defining rules. The operational semantics is based on an optimal evaluation strategy [4]—a conservative extension of lazy functional programming and logic programming.

A Curry program consists of the definition of data types (introducing data *constructors*) and *functions* or *operations* on these types. For instance, the data types for Boolean values and polymorphic lists are as follows:

```
data Bool = False | True
data List a = [] | a : List a    -- [a] denotes "List a"
```

A *value* is an expression without defined operations. As mentioned in Sect. 1, Curry allows the definition of non-deterministic operations with the choice operator "?" so that the expression "True ? False" has two values: True and False. Using non-deterministic operations as arguments might cause a semantical ambiguity which has to be fixed. For instance, consider the operations

```
xor True  x = not x        not True  = False
xor False x = x            not False = True

xorSelf x = xor x x        aBool = True ? False
```

and the expression "xorSelf aBool". If we interpret this program as a term rewriting system, we could have the derivation

```
xorSelf aBool  →   xor aBool aBool   →   xor True aBool
               →   xor True False    →   not False     →   True
```

leading to the unintended result True. Note that this result cannot be obtained if we use a strict strategy where arguments are evaluated prior to the function calls. In order to avoid dependencies on the evaluation strategies and exclude such unintended results, González-Moreno et al. [17] proposed the rewriting logic CRWL as a logical (execution- and strategy-independent) foundation for declarative programming with non-strict and non-deterministic operations. CRWL specifies the *call-time choice* semantics [22], where values of the arguments of an operation are determined before the operation is evaluated. This can be enforced in

---

[1] Variables and function names usually start with lowercase letters and the names of type and data constructors start with an uppercase letter. The application of f to e is denoted by juxtaposition ("$f\ e$").

a lazy strategy by sharing actual arguments. For instance, the expression above can be lazily evaluated provided that all occurrences of `aBool` are shared so that all of them reduce either to `True` or to `False` consistently. Thus, sharing is not an option to support an efficient evaluation, but it is required for semantical reasons.

Fortunately, sharing is not an extra burden but already provided by implementations of lazy languages in order to avoid duplication of work. To avoid re-evaluations of identical subexpressions, e.g., the subexpression $f\ e$ in `xorSelf` $(f\ e)$ where f might cause an expensive computation, the two occurrences of x in the right-hand side of the `xorSelf` rule are *shared*. This can be achieved by a graph represention of expressions so that all occurrences of x refer to the same graph node. Hence, if $f\ e$ is evaluated as the first argument of `xor` to some value v, the node containing f is replaced by v so that the second argument of `xor` also refers to v. This "update-in-place" of evaluated function calls is essential for lazy languages and also required to ensure the optimality of lazy strategies for functional logic languages [4].

Formally, we can consider programs as graph rewriting systems [28] so that rewrite steps are graph replacements. In order to simplify our presentation, we use the idea to represent sharing by `let` expressions, similarly to Lauchbury's natural semantics for lazy evaluation [23]. This is also used to specify the operational semantics of functional logic languages [1]. Bindings of `let` expressions are stored in a heap so that updates of function nodes are represented as heap updates. Instead of repeating the details of [1], we show the possible evaluations of `xorSelf aBool` in this heap model. Here, the heap is shown on the left, evaluations with the same heap are written in the same line, and new evaluation tasks caused by non-deterministic choices are indented:

$$
\begin{array}{lll}
[\,] & \texttt{let x = aBool in xorSelf x} & (1) \\
[x \mapsto \texttt{aBool}] & \to\ \texttt{xorSelf x} \to \texttt{xor x x} & (2) \\
[x \mapsto \texttt{True ? False}] & \to\ \texttt{xor x x} & (3) \\
\quad [x \mapsto \texttt{True}] & \texttt{xor x x} \to \texttt{not x} \to \boxed{\texttt{False}} & (4) \\
\quad [x \mapsto \texttt{False}] & \texttt{xor x x} \to \texttt{x} \to \boxed{\texttt{False}} & (5)
\end{array}
$$

In line (2), the `let` binding is moved into the heap. The function call in this binding is evaluated and updated in (3). Since this is a choice, a new evaluation task is established for each alternative. Thanks to the sharing of the value of x, the unintended value `True` is not computed as a result. Since a heap can be considered as another representation of a graph structure, we use heaps and graphs interchangeably.

3   Pull-Tabbing

If non-deterministic choices are implemented by backtracking, as in Prolog, one has to reason about the influence of the search strategy to the success of an evaluation—a non-trivial task in the presence of a lazy evaluation strategy. To support better search strategies, like breadth-first or parallel search, all non-deterministic choices should be represented in a single (graph) structure so that one can easily switch between different computation branches. As discussed in Sect. 1, pull-tabbing [2,3] has been used in implementations supporting advanced search strategies. A *pull-tab step* moves a choice occurring in a demanded argument of an operation outside this operation: if f demands the value of its single argument, then

$$f\ (e_1\ ?\ e_2)\quad\rightarrow\quad (f\ e_1)\ ?\ (f\ e_2)$$

is a pull-tab step.

The nice aspects of pull-tabbing are its operational completeness [3] and the locality of steps. Iterated pull-tab steps move choices towards the root:

```
not (not (True ? False))  →  not ((not True) ? (not False))
                          →  (not (not True)) ? (not (not False))
```

A choice at the root of an expression leads to two new expressions that must be evaluated and might lead to two result values. Since pull-tabbing does not fix some search strategy, it is assumed that these alternative expressions are evaluated by different computation *tasks*. Conceptually, an entire computation consists of a set of tasks where each task evaluates some node of a graph. In this example, the new tasks evaluate the expressions not (not True) and not(not False), respectively.

Pull-tab steps as described so far are not sufficient to correctly implement a non-strict functional logic language like Curry. As discussed in Sect. 2, the call-time choice semantics requires to share the values of non-deterministic arguments in a computation. We can implement this requirement by adding identifiers to choices and associating a "fingerprint" [11] to each task. A *fingerprint* is a (partial) mapping from choice identifiers to choice alternatives (*Left* or *Right*). When a task reaches a choice at the root, it proceeds as follows:

- If the fingerprint of the task contains a selection for this choice, select the corresponding branch of this choice.
- Otherwise, create two new tasks for the left and right alternative where the fingerprint is extended for this choice with L and R, respectively.

With this refinement of pull-tabbing, we obtain the following evaluation of a variation of "xorSelf aBool" (where the fingerprint of the task is written on the left and the heap, which is always [x ↦ True ?₁ False], is omitted):

$$
\begin{array}{ll}
[] & \texttt{xor x x} \rightarrow (\texttt{xor True x}) \ ?_1 \ (\texttt{xor False x}) \\
[1/L] & \texttt{xor True x} \rightarrow \texttt{not x} \rightarrow (\texttt{not True}) \ ?_1 \ (\texttt{not False}) \\
[1/L] & \rightarrow \texttt{not True} \rightarrow \boxed{\texttt{False}} \\
[1/R] & \texttt{xor False x} \rightarrow \texttt{x} \rightarrow \texttt{True} \ ?_1 \ \texttt{False} \\
[1/R] & \rightarrow \boxed{\texttt{False}}
\end{array}
$$

Thanks to fingerprints, only values which are correct w.r.t. the call-time choice semantics are produced [3].

Unfortunately, pull-tabbing has some performance problems. In contrast to backtracking, where a non-deterministic choice is implemented by selecting one branch and proceed with this selection until failure or success, pull-tabbing moves each non-deterministic choice up to the root of the expression under evaluation. Hence, the consistency of choices is checked only for choices at the root, i.e., outside function calls. This has the operational consequence that *each* access to a non-deterministic expression leads to a stepwise shifting of choices towards the root. Thus, multiple accesses to a same non-deterministic expression multiplies the execution time. For instance, consider a function

$$f \ x \ = \ C[x, \ldots, x] \tag{1}$$

where the right-hand side is (or evaluates to) an expression containing n occurrences of the argument x (represented by the context C). Now consider the evaluation of $f(e_1 \ ? \ e_2)$. Whenever some occurrence of x in C is demanded in this evaluation, the choice occurring in the actual argument is moved up to the root by pull-tabbing. Hence, if all n occurrences of x in C are demanded at depth d, approximately $n \cdot d$ pull-tab steps are performed (and most of the resulting choice nodes are omitted at the end due to fingerprinting). In contrast, backtracking is more efficient since it selects one alternative for the first occurrence of x and then simply uses this alternative for all subsequent occurrences of x.

4   Memoized Pull-Tabbing

In this section we present an improvement of pull-tabbing which avoids the performance problems discussed above.

4.1   The Basic Scheme

In principle, the duplication of choices is necessary due to shared subexpressions which are evaluated by different tasks. In contrast to purely functional programming, it would be wrong to update graph nodes of such expressions by their results if they occur in a non-deterministic context. As a solution to this problem, we propose to store "task-specific" updates in the graph, i.e., instead of updating graph nodes by their computed results, we keep the graph nodes but memorize results already computed by some task for a function node. When a task has to evaluate a function node again due to sharing, it directly uses an already computed result.

In order to implement this idea, each task evaluating some expression (subgraph) has a unique identifier (e.g., a number), also called *task identifier*. To store task-specific updates, each graph node representing a function call contains a (partial) map tr, called *task result map*, from task identifiers to graph nodes.

To avoid repeated pull-tab steps, pull-tab steps are not performed for choices that already contain a selection in the fingerprint of the task. In this case, we proceed with the selected branch but have to remember, by using the task result map, that computed results are valid only for this branch. To be more precise, consider a node n representing some function call $f(e_1?_ce_2)$, where f demands its argument. This node is evaluated by the task with identifier i as follows:

- If task i contains no selection for c in its fingerprint, a standard pull-tab step is performed, i.e., two new nodes $n_1 = f\ e_1$ and $n_2 = f\ e_2$ are created and n is updated to $n_1?_cn_2$.
- If task i contains a selection for c, say L, it would be wrong to update node n to $f\ e_1$ due to possible sharing of n. Instead, a new node $n' = f\ e_1$ is created and $n.tr$ is updated with $n.tr(i) = n'$.

This strategy has the consequence that only the first occurrence of a choice in a computation is moved to the root by iterated pull-tab steps. Since a choice at the root causes a splitting of the current task into two new tasks evaluating the left and right alternative, respectively, this choice, when evaluated again due to sharing, has a selection in the fingerprint so that this selection is immediately taken and stored in the task result map.

Since function calls can be nested, the task result map must be considered for any function call, i.e., also those without a choice in an argument. Thus, when a task with identifier i evaluates some function node n, it checks whether $n.tr(i)$ is defined:

- If $n.tr(i) = n'$, then n' is evaluated instead of n.
- If $n.tr(i)$ is undefined, n is evaluated to some node n' and $n.tr$ is updated with $n.tr(i) = n'$.

Hence, if node n is shared so that task i has to evaluate n again, the already evaluated result is taken.

This evaluation scheme requires a bit more time when function nodes are accessed but avoids the expensive duplication of non-deterministic computations with pure pull-tabbing. We call this improved strategy *memoized pull-tabbing* (*MPT*).

Memoized pull-tabbing can reduce the complexity of non-deterministic computations. For instance, consider again function f defined by rule (1) in Sect. 3. When the expression `let x = `$e_1?_1e_2$` in `f` x` is evaluated, rule (1) is applied and eventually the first occurrence of x is evaluated by a pull-tab step. This leads (by iterated pull-tab steps) to the expression

`let x = `$e_1\ ?_1\ e_2$` in `$C[e_1,x,\ldots,x]\ ?_1\ C[e_2,x,\ldots,x]$

The left and right alternative are further evaluated by two tasks T_1 and T_2 having an L and R selection for choice 1, respectively. Task T_1 evaluates all further occurrences of x by selecting e_1 and setting the task result maps of the parent nodes to the results computed with this selection. Hence, instead of $n \cdot d$ pull-tab steps with pure pull-tabbing, MPT performs only d pull-tab steps and $n - 1$ "selection" steps for each task T_1 and T_2 to evaluate the initial expression.

Before presenting and evaluating an implementation of MPT, we propose some refinements which will lead to our final MPT strategy.

4.2   Refinements for Deterministic Computations

In typical application programs, large parts of an evaluation are *deterministic computations*, i.e., computations where choice nodes do not occur. Similarly, a *deterministic expression* is an expression whose evaluation does not demand the evaluation of a choice. Since a reasonable implementation of a functional logic language should support efficient deterministic computations, we present two improvements of our basic MPT strategy for this purpose.

Our first refinement tries to avoid the use of the task result map tr in nodes whenever it is not necessary, in particular, for deterministic computations. For this purpose, each graph node n has an *owner task* (ot), i.e., $n.ot$ is the identifier of the task that created this node. For the initial expression, the owner task of all nodes is the identifier of the main task. When a rule is applied, i.e., a function call is replaced by the right-hand side of a program rule, the owner task of the nodes created for the right-hand side is identical to the owner task of the root of the left-hand side. In case of a pull-tab step

$$f\ (e_1\ ?\ e_2)\quad \rightarrow\quad (f\ e_1)\ ?\ (f\ e_2)$$

the owner tasks of the new function calls $f\ e_1$ and $f\ e_2$ are the identifiers of the new tasks that will evaluate the left and right alternative, respectively.

In order to compare the owner tasks of nodes, we assume a partial ordering on task identifiers. Note that new tasks are created when a choice appears at the root. In this case the current task t is split into two new tasks t_1 and t_2 which evaluate the left and right alternative of the choice, respectively. We call t *parent* of t_1 and t_2. If i, i_1, i_2 are the identifiers of t, t_1, t_2, respectively, then we assume that $i < i_1$ and $i < i_2$. We call node n_1 *younger* than n_2 if $n_1.ot > n_2.ot$.

If the current task evaluates some choice $n = e_1?_c e_2$ and the fingerprint of the task already contains a decision for this choice, we follow this decision instead of pushing the choice towards the root by a pull-tab step, as described above. Now we refine the basic scheme by considering the owner tasks. Assume that i is the identifier of the current task, its fingerprint selects e_1 for choice c, and there is the parent node $n' = f\ n$ (for simplicity, we consider only unary functions in this discussion). We distinguish the following cases:

1. If $i > n'.ot$, then $n'.tr(i)$ is set to a new node $n'' = f\ e_1$ with $n''.ot = i$ and the evaluation proceeds with node n''.
2. Otherwise ($i = n'.ot$), node n' is updated in place such that $n' = f\ e_1$.

Next consider the situation that there is some function node $n = f\ a$ and the argument a has been evaluated to a'.

1. If a' is younger than n, the argument has been evaluated to some value which is valid only in the new task which created a'. Instead of updating n in place, $n.tr(a'.ot)$ is set to a new node $n' = f\ a'$ with $n'.ot = a'.ot$ and the evaluation proceeds with node n' instead of n.
2. Otherwise (a' is not younger than n), the value computed for a is valid for n so that n is updated in place such that $n = f\ a'$.

Thus, for deterministic computations, which are performed in a single task (tasks are created only for non-deterministic steps), the task result maps are not used at all.

A further refinement exploits the tree structure of tasks. An *ancestor* of a task is either its parent or the parent of some ancestor of the task. Consider the case that we have to evaluate some function node n in a task identified by i:

1. If $n.tr(i)$ is defined, then task i already evaluated node n so that we can proceed with $n.tr(i)$ instead of n.
2. If $n.tr(i)$ is not defined and j is a parent of i so that $n.tr(j) = n'$, then n' is also a valid result of n so that we can proceed with n'. Hence, we follow the ancestor chain of i to find the first ancestor k such that $n.tr(k)$ is defined.
3. Otherwise (there is no ancestor j of i with $n.tr(j)$ defined), we evaluate n.

Note that the owner task of nodes changes in a computation only if some choice node is evaluated. In case of a pull-tab step, the new nodes are younger than the choice node. If there is some decision for the choice w.r.t. the fingerprint of the current task, we commit to the selected branch and set the owner task of this selection to the current task. An interesting consequence of this strategy is that the owner tasks of nodes in a computation are not changed when choice nodes do not occur in this computation. In particular, deterministic computations without occurrences of choice nodes are always evaluated in place—independently of the task which evaluated them. This has the effect that deterministic expressions are evaluated at most once, even if they are shared among non-deterministic branches. This property, also called *sharing across non-determinism* [15], is an important feature of the pull-tab strategy. Consider an expression

```
let x = e in C₁[x] ? C₂[x]
```

where e is a deterministic expression and the value of x is demanded in both $C_1[x]$ and $C_2[x]$. Then e will be evaluated only once since the task evaluating $C_1[x]$ will replace e by its result so that this result is available for the task evaluating $C_2[x]$. In contrast, an implementation based on backtracking would evaluate e two times since the evaluation of e by the task evaluating $C_1[x]$ will be undone before evaluating $C_2[x]$. Note that this is not only a problem of backtracking. For instance, the approach to implement call-time choice with purely functional programming features presented in [16] also reports the lack of sharing across non-determinism.

5 Implementation

In order to evaluate our ideas, we implemented MPT in Julia[2], a high-level dynamic programming language. We used Julia due to its direct support of dynamic data structures, garbage collection, and higher-order features. By exploiting the intermediate language ICurry [9], the compiler from ICurry to

---

[2] https://julialang.org/.

Julia is approximately 300 lines of Curry code. Furthermore, the run-time system, responsible to implement the computation graph, pull-tab steps, computation tasks with various search strategies, and some more aspects, consists of approximately 300 lines of Julia code. Thus, this implementation, called "JuCS" (Julia Curry System[3]), is a proof of concept which could also be implemented, with more effort and probably more efficiently, in other imperative languages, like C. In the following, we sketch some aspects of this implementation.

Apart from the memoized pull-tabbing strategy, the implementation has many similarities to Sprite [11]. Expressions are represented as a graph structure. To distinguish different kinds of graph nodes (function, constructor, choice, failure, etc.), each node has a tag. Furthermore, a node contains an integer value (choice identifier, constructor index, etc.), the identifier of the owner task, an array of references to argument nodes, a code reference in case of function nodes, and a task result map (a Julia dictionary with task identifiers as keys and node references as values). The run-time system works on a queue of tasks where each task contains a unique number, the root node evaluated by this task, the fingerprint, and the identifiers of the parent tasks. With these data structures, the run-time system evaluates expressions, as described above, by computing the head normal form of the root node of the current task. If this yields a choice node, two new tasks are created with extended fingerprints. In case of depth-first search, these tasks are added at the front of the task queue, while they are added at the back in case of breadth-first search.

Free variables and their bindings require a non-trivial implementation with non-deterministic value generator operations in a pure pull-tabbing implementation [14]. Our MPT strategy allows a much simpler implementation. Instead of representing free variables as value generators (as in [6]), JuCS has a "free" tag for nodes where the task result map is used to store task-specific bindings for free variables. Hence, free variables are handled as efficient as in Prolog implementations while still allowing more flexible search strategies.

In order to compare the different run-time models (MPT, pull-tabbing, backtracking) inside our implementation, JuCS contains also two alternative run-time systems implementing pure pull-tabbing and backtracking. The pull-tabbing system is a reduced variant of the standard run-time system. The backtracking system uses ideas from Prolog implementations, in particular, the improved backtracking and trailing mechanism of Warren's Abstract Machine [29] to reduce the amount of stored backtrack information.

6 Benchmarks

Memoized pull-tabbing requires more effort at run time than pure pull-tabbing due to the tests when evaluating or updating a function node in the computation graph. Thus, it is interesting to see whether this pays off in practice. Therefore, we executed a set of benchmarks with our new implementation and

---

[3] Available at https://github.com/cau-placc/julia-curry.

Table 1. Evaluating different run-time systems of JuCS

Program	MPT	pull-tab	backtrack
nrev	2.37 s	2.29 s	7.09 s
takPeano	12.04 s	11.84 s	31.78 s
addNum2	0.46 s	6.21 s	0.39 s
addNum5	1.61 s	47.69 s	1.26 s
select50	0.05 s	4.18 s	0.14 s
select75	0.10 s	24.10 s	0.31 s
select100	0.18 s	111.47 s	0.55 s

Table 2. Effect of sharing across non-determinism

Program	MPT	pull-tab	backtrack
sort1	9.83 s	9.96 s	15.47 s
sort2	9.84 s	9.73 s	155.64 s

compared the execution times[4] of the different run-time systems provided with this implementation. The results are summarized in Table 1.

The first two examples[5] are purely deterministic programs: nrev is the quadratic naive reverse algorithm on a list with 4096 elements and takPeano is a highly recursive function on naturals [26] applied to arguments (24,16,8), where numbers and arithmetic operations are in Peano representation. addNum2 and addNum5 non-deterministically choose a number (out of 2000) and add it two and five times, respectively. select$n$ non-deterministically selects an element in a list of length n and sums up the element and the list without the selected element.

As one can see from the direct comparison to pure pull-tabbing, the overhead caused by the additional checks required for memoization is limited and immediately pays off when non-deterministic expressions are shared, which is often the case in applications involving non-determinism.

It is interesting to note that the backtracking strategy is less efficient than MPT, although MPT supports more flexible search strategies. This might be due to the fact that backtracking has to check, for each reduction step, whether this step has to be remembered in order to undo it in case of backtracking.

As already discussed, backtracking has another disadvantage: deterministic computations are not shared across non-deterministic computations. This has the unfortunate consequence that a client using some algorithm of a library has to know whether this algorithm is implemented with non-deterministic features, since arguments might be evaluated multiple times with backtracking. To show this effect, consider the deterministic insertion sort operation isort, the non-

---

[4] All benchmarks were executed on a Linux machine running Ubuntu 18.04 with an Intel Core i7-85550U (1.8 GHz) processor.

[5] The actual programs are available with the implementation described in Sect. 5.

Table 3. Relative execution times of BFS vs. DFS

Example	KiCS2 (BFS/DFS)	JuCS (BFS/DFS)
addNum2	2.18	1.02
addNum5	1.58	1.00
select50	1.03	1.00
select100	1.28	1.04
permsort	4.46	1.11

deterministic permutation sort operation `psort`, and the infinite list of all prime numbers `primes` together with the following definitions (this example is inspired from [13]):

```
sort1 = isort [primes!!303, primes!!302, primes!!301, primes!!300]
sort2 = psort [primes!!303, primes!!302, primes!!301, primes!!300]
```

In principle, one would expect that the execution time of `sort1` is almost equal to the time to execute `sort2` since the time to sort a four-element list is neglectable. However, implementations based on backtracking evaluate the primes occurring in `sort2` multiple times, as can be seen by the run times shown in Table 2.

We already emphasized the fact that pull-tabbing supports flexible search strategies. Since all non-deterministic values of an expression are represented in one structure, different search strategies can be implemented as traversals on this structure. For instance, KiCS2 evaluates each expression to a tree of its values so that the top-level computation collecting all values can be defined as a traversal on this tree [13]. Our implementation uses a queue of tasks so that search strategies can be implemented as specific strategies to put and get tasks to and from the queue, respectively (as sketched above). The practical behavior of search strategies in KiCS2 was analyzed in [20] (since then, breadth-first search became the default strategy for KiCS2). Table 3 shows that MPT has an even better behavior since, in contrast to pure pull-tabbing, it is not necessary to move all choices to the root in order to build a tree of all values. Here, we also added the classical permutation sort example since it showed a larger slowdown of breadth-first search in [20].

7 Related Work

In this section we review other approaches to implement functional logic languages and relate our proposal to them.

Early approaches to implement functional logic languages exploited Prolog's backtracking strategy for non-deterministic computations [5,24]. By adding a mechanism to implement demand-driven evaluation, one can use Prolog as a target language, as done in PAKCS [19] and TOY [25]. The usage of Prolog yields also a direct support for free variables. However, such implementations suffer from the operational incompleteness of the backtracking strategy.

Pull-tabbing supports more flexible search strategies by representing choices as data. The theoretical properties are investigated in [3]. On the practical side, pull-tabbing is useful to implement non-determinism in a deterministic target language. For instance, ViaLOIS [12] uses pull-tabbing to translate Curry programs into Haskell and OCaml programs, respectively. ICurry [9] is an intermediate language intended to translate Curry programs into imperative target languages. It has been used to translate Curry to LLVM code [11] and to C or Python programs [30]. The operational semantics of ICurry is specified in [9] by an abstract machine which performs pull-tab steps and uses a graph structure to represent expressions with sharing and a queue of tasks, where each task has its own fingerprint to implement the selection of consistent choices.

The Curry compiler KiCS2 [13] is based on pull-tabbing and compiles Curry programs into a purely functional Haskell programs. Non-determinism is implemented by representing choices as data terms so that Curry expressions are evaluated to choice trees. Pull-tab steps are encoded as rules for choice terms. Values are extracted from choice trees by traversing them with fingerprints. Hence, KiCS2 implements non-determinism in a modular way: any expression is evaluated to a choice tree representation of all its values, and there is a separate operation which extracts correct values from the choice tree structure. Therefore, KiCS2 implements various search strategies as different tree traversal strategies, and infinite search spaces (choice trees) do not cause problems due to Haskell's lazy evaluation strategy.

Since KiCS2 suffers from the performance problems of pure pull-tabbing, an eager evaluation of demanded non-deterministic subexpressions is proposed in [18]. An automatic program transformation implementing this optimization is based on a demand analysis. However, this approach does not work for arbitrary programs since a precise demand analysis for complex data structures is non-trivial and not yet available for functional logic programs. Therefore, it is an interesting question for future work whether our MPT scheme can be combined with the purely functional implementation approach of KiCS2.

Sharing across non-determinism describes the property that deterministic subexpressions shared in different non-deterministic branches are evaluated at most once. This is usually not the case in implementations based on backtracking. As emphasized in [15], pull-tabbing easily ensures this property if the target language implements sharing for common subexpressions, as in our implementation or in lazy functional target languages [13,15].

An approach to support functional logic programming features as in Curry in a purely functional language is a library for non-deterministic computations with (explicit) sharing [16]. The key idea of this library is to translate non-deterministic computations into monadic computations that manipulate a *thunk store*. The thunk store holds either unevaluated computations or their results, which may again contain unevaluated arguments, and is closely related to the heap described in Sect. 2. The library provides an explicit `share` operation to allow the sharing of computations. Shared computations are initially entered unevaluated into the thunk store and only the demand for a computation triggers its evaluation. If a computation is non-deterministic, the thunk store is updated with the corresponding result independently in each branch. All subse-

Table 4. Comparing properties of implementation strategies

	Backtracking	Explicit sharing	Pull tabbing	MPT
Flexible search strategies	−	+	+	+
Free variables	+	−	−	+
Sharing across non-determinism	−	−	+	+
Sharing non-determinism	+	+	−	+

quent uses of the shared computation within one computation branch then reuse the updated result in the thunk store. Although shared results are reused in one computation branch if demanded more than once, the library does not support sharing across non-determinism because shared computations are evaluated independently in different branches. Due to the fact that the implementation relies on the type class `MonadPlus`, different search strategies can be exploited depending on the concrete instance of `MonadPlus`. Furthermore, the library has no direct support of free variables and can only emulate them by using non-deterministic generators [6].

Table 4 compares the properties of the various approaches to implement demand-driven non-deterministic computations discussed above. "Flexible search strategies" means whether only one or a number of different search strategies are supported. "Free variables" denotes a direct support of free variables. This is not the case for explicit sharing and pull-tabbing, since they require a simulation of free variables by non-deterministic generator operations and non-trivial techniques to obtain the effect of binding free variables through unification [14]. "Sharing across non-determinism" describes the aforementioned ability to reuse already computed results of deterministic subexpressions in different branches of non-deterministic computations. "Sharing non-determinism" means that the results of already evaluated non-deterministic subexpressions are re-used when these subexpressions are shared. As one can see, our new MPT strategy is the only implementation which combines all these properties. As shown by our benchmarks, this has a positive effect on the efficiency of MPT on a range of different application scenarios.

8   Conclusions

The efficient implementation of functional logic programming languages is still a challenge due to the combination of advanced declarative programming concepts. In order to free the programmer from considering details about the concrete evaluation strategy, it is desirable to support operationally complete strategies which ensure that values are computed whenever they exist. This can be obtained by representing the complete state with all branches of a non-deterministic computation in one data structure. Pull-tabbing is a simple and local transformation to deal with non-deterministic choices. However, pull-tabbing has the risk to duplicate work during evaluation. In this paper we proposed a significant improvement by adding a kind of memoization to pull-tabbing. As we demonstrated by our benchmarks, this improved evaluation mechanism does not cause much overhead, is often faster than backtracking, and can dramatically improve pure pull-tabbing. Morever, it keeps all the positive properties of pull-tabbing: application of various search strategies and sharing across non-determinism. Our prototypical implementation showed that it can also be implemented with modest efforts: Curry programs can be compiled by using the already existing intermediate language ICurry in a straightforward manner, and the run-time system is quite compact. Thus, it is an ideal model to implement multi-paradigm declarative languages also with other target languages, e.g., to integrate declarative programming in applications written in other imperative languages.

Nevertheless, there is room for future work. For instance, one could try to identify non-shared subexpressions, e.g., by some sharing or linearity analysis, to avoid run-time checking of memoized data. Another interesting question is whether it is possible to implement the presented ideas in a purely functional manner so that one can use them to improve existing approaches like KiCS2 [14] or the library for explicit sharing [16].

References

1. Albert, E., Hanus, M., Huch, F., Oliver, J., Vidal, G.: Operational semantics for declarative multi-paradigm languages. J. Symb. Comput. **40**(1), 795–829 (2005)
2. Alqaddoumi, A., Antoy, S., Fischer, S., Reck, F.: The pull-tab transformation. In: Proceedings of the Third International Workshop on Graph Computation Models, Enschede, The Netherlands, pp. 127–132 (2010). http://gcm2010.imag.fr/pages/gcm2010-preproceedings.pdf
3. Antoy, S.: On the correctness of pull-tabbing. Theory Pract. Logic Program. **11**(4–5), 713–730 (2011)
4. Antoy, S., Echahed, R., Hanus, M.: A needed narrowing strategy. J. ACM **47**(4), 776–822 (2000)
5. Antoy, S., Hanus, M.: Compiling multi-paradigm declarative programs into prolog. In: Kirchner, H., Ringeissen, C. (eds.) FroCoS 2000. LNCS (LNAI), vol. 1794, pp. 171–185. Springer, Heidelberg (2000). https://doi.org/10.1007/10720084_12
6. Antoy, S., Hanus, M.: Overlapping rules and logic variables in functional logic programs. In: Etalle, S., Truszczyński, M. (eds.) ICLP 2006. LNCS, vol. 4079, pp. 87–101. Springer, Heidelberg (2006). https://doi.org/10.1007/11799573_9
7. Antoy, S., Hanus, M.: Functional logic programming. Commun. ACM **53**(4), 74–85 (2010)
8. Antoy, S., Hanus, M.: Contracts and specifications for functional logic programming. In: Russo, C., Zhou, N.-F. (eds.) PADL 2012. LNCS, vol. 7149, pp. 33–47. Springer, Heidelberg (2012). https://doi.org/10.1007/978-3-642-27694-1_4
9. Antoy, S., Hanus, M., Jost, A., Libby, S.: ICurry. In: Hofstedt, P., Abreu, S., John, U., Kuchen, H., Seipel, D. (eds.) INAP/WLP/WFLP -2019. LNCS (LNAI), vol. 12057, pp. 286–307. Springer, Cham (2020). https://doi.org/10.1007/978-3-030-46714-2_18
10. Antoy, S., Hanus, M., Liu, J., Tolmach, A.: A virtual machine for functional logic computations. In: Grelck, C., Huch, F., Michaelson, G.J., Trinder, P. (eds.) IFL 2004. LNCS, vol. 3474, pp. 108–125. Springer, Heidelberg (2005). https://doi.org/10.1007/11431664_7

11. Antoy, S., Jost, A.: A new functional-logic compiler for curry: SPRITE. In: Hermenegildo, M.V., Lopez-Garcia, P. (eds.) LOPSTR 2016. LNCS, vol. 10184, pp. 97–113. Springer, Cham (2017). https://doi.org/10.1007/978-3-319-63139-4_6

12. Antoy, S., Peters, A.: Compiling a functional logic language: *the basic scheme*. In: Schrijvers, T., Thiemann, P. (eds.) FLOPS 2012. LNCS, vol. 7294, pp. 17–31. Springer, Heidelberg (2012). https://doi.org/10.1007/978-3-642-29822-6_5

13. Braßel, B., Hanus, M., Peemöller, B., Reck, F.: KiCS2: a new compiler from curry to Haskell. In: Kuchen, H. (ed.) WFLP 2011. LNCS, vol. 6816, pp. 1–18. Springer, Heidelberg (2011). https://doi.org/10.1007/978-3-642-22531-4_1

14. Braßel, B., Hanus, M., Peemöller, B., Reck, F.: Implementing equational constraints in a functional language. In: Sagonas, K. (ed.) PADL 2013. LNCS, vol. 7752, pp. 125–140. Springer, Heidelberg (2013). https://doi.org/10.1007/978-3-642-45284-0_9

15. Braßel, B., Huch, F.: On a tighter integration of functional and logic programming. In: Shao, Z. (ed.) APLAS 2007. LNCS, vol. 4807, pp. 122–138. Springer, Heidelberg (2007). https://doi.org/10.1007/978-3-540-76637-7_9

16. Fischer, S., Kiselyov, O., Shan, C.: Purely functional lazy nondeterministic programming. J. Funct. Program. **21**(4&5), 413–465 (2011)

17. González-Moreno, J.C., Hortalá-González, M.T., López-Fraguas, F.J., Rodríguez-Artalejo, M.: An approach to declarative programming based on a rewriting logic. J. Log. Program. **40**, 47–87 (1999)

18. Hanus, M.: Improving lazy non-deterministic computations by demand analysis. In: Technical Communications of the 28th International Conference on Logic Programming, vol. 17, pp. 130–143. Leibniz International Proceedings in Informatics (LIPIcs) (2012)

19. Hanus, M., et al.: PAKCS: The Portland Aachen Kiel Curry System (2018). http://www.informatik.uni-kiel.de/~pakcs/

20. Hanus, M., Peemöller, B., Reck, F.: Search strategies for functional logic programming. In: Proceedings of the 5th Working Conference on Programming Languages (ATPS 2012). LNI, vol. 199, pp. 61–74. Springer (2012). https://dl.gi.de/20.500.12116/18376

21. Hanus, M. (ed.) Curry: an integrated functional logic language (vers. 0.9.0) (2016). http://www.curry-lang.org

22. Hussmann, H.: Nondeterministic algebraic specifications and nonconfluent term rewriting. J. Log. Program. **12**, 237–255 (1992)

23. Launchbury, J.: A natural semantics for lazy evaluation. In: Proceedings of the 20th ACM Symposium on Principles of Programming Languages (POPL 1993), pp. 144–154. ACM Press (1993)

24. Loogen, R., Fraguas, F.L., Artalejo, M.R.: A demand driven computation strategy for lazy narrowing. In: Bruynooghe, M., Penjam, J. (eds.) PLILP 1993. LNCS, vol. 714, pp. 184–200. Springer, Heidelberg (1993). https://doi.org/10.1007/3-540-57186-8_79

25. López Fraguas, F.J., Sánchez Hernández, J.: *TOY*: a multiparadigm declarative system. In: Narendran, P., Rusinowitch, M. (eds.) RTA 1999. LNCS, vol. 1631, pp. 244–247. Springer, Heidelberg (1999). https://doi.org/10.1007/3-540-48685-2_19

26. Partain, W.: The nofib benchmark suite of Haskell programs. In: Launchbury, J., Sansom, P. (eds.) Functional Programming, Glasgow 1992. Workshops in Computing, pp. 195–202. Springer, London (1993). https://doi.org/10.1007/978-1-4471-3215-8_17

27. Peyton Jones, S. (ed.): Haskell 98 Language and Libraries-The Revised Report. Cambridge University Press (2003)

28. Plump, D.: Term graph rewriting. In: Ehrig, H., Engels, G., Kreowski, H.-J., Rozenberg, G. (eds.) Handbook of Graph Grammars and Computing by Graph Transformation, Applications, Languages and Tools, vol. 2, pp. 3–61. World Scientific (1999)

29. Warren, D.H.D.: An abstract Prolog instruction set. Technical note 309, SRI International, Stanford (1983)

30. Wittorf, M.A.: Generic translation of Curry programs into imperative programs (in German). Master's thesis, Kiel University (2018)

Effectiveness of Annotation-Based Static Type Inference

Isabel Wingen and Philipp Körner(✉) ⓘ

Institut für Informatik, Universität Düsseldorf,
Universit ätsstr. 1, 40225 Düsseldorf, Germany
{isabel.wingen,p.koerner}@uni-duesseldorf.de

Abstract. Benefits of static type systems are well-known: they offer guarantees that no type error will occur during runtime and, inherently, inferred types serve as documentation on how functions are called. On the other hand, many type systems have to limit expressiveness of the language because, in general, it is undecidable whether a given program is correct regarding types. Another concern that was not addressed so far is that, for logic programming languages such as Prolog, it is impossible to distinguish between intended and unintended failure and, worse, intended and unintended success without additional annotations.

In this paper, we elaborate on and discuss the aforementioned issues. As an alternative, we present a static type analysis which is based on *plspec*. Instead of ensuring full type-safety, we aim to statically identify type errors on a best-effort basis without limiting the expressiveness of Prolog programs. Finally, we evaluate our approach on real-world code featured in the SWI community packages and a large project implementing a model checker.

Keywords: Prolog · Static verification · Optional type system · Data specification

1 Introduction

Dynamic type systems often enable type errors during development. Generally, this is not too much of an issue as errors usually get caught early by test cases or REPL-driven development. Prolog programs however do not follow patterns prevalent in other programming paradigms. Exceptions are thrown rarely and execution is resumed at some prior point via backtracking instead before queries ultimately fail (or succeed due to the wrong reason). This renders it cumbersome to identify type errors, their location and when they occur.

There has been broad research on type systems offering a guarantee about the absence of type errors (briefly discussed in Sect. 2). Yet, in dynamic programming languages such as Prolog, a complete well-typing of arbitrary programs is undecidable [14]. Thus, in order for the type system to work, the expressiveness of the language often is limited. This hinders adaptation to existing code severely, and, as a consequence, type errors are often ignored in larger projects.

© Springer Nature Switzerland AG 2021
M. Hanus and C. Sacerdoti Coen (Eds.): WFLP 2020, LNCS 12560, pp. 74–93, 2021.
https://doi.org/10.1007/978-3-030-75333-7_5

At DECLARE'17, we presented *plspec* [7], a type system that uses annotations in order to insert run-time type checks (cf. Sect. 3). During discussions, the point was raised that some type checks could be made statically even with optional types. This paper thus contributes the following:

- A type analysis tool usable for *any* unmodified Prolog program. It handles a proper "any" type and is extensible for any Prolog dialect (Sect. 4).
- An empirical evaluation of the amount of inferred types using this tool (Sect. 5).
- Automatic inference and generation of pre- and postconditions of *plspec*.

2   A Note on Type Systems and Related Work

Static type systems have a huge success story, mostly in functional programming languages like Haskell [6] but also in some Prolog derivatives such as Mercury [4], which uses type and mode information in order to achieve major performance boosts. Even similar dynamic languages such as Erlang include a type specification language [5]. Many static type systems for logic programming languages have been presented [13] including the seminal works of Mycroft and O'Keefe [12], which also influenced Typed Prolog [8], and a pluggable type system for Yap and SWI-Prolog [16].

All type systems have some common foundations yet usually vary in expressiveness. Some type systems *suggest* type annotations for functions or predicates, some *require* annotations of all predicates or those of which the type cannot be inferred automatically to a satisfactory level. Yet, type checking of logic programs is, in general, undecidable [14]. This renders only three feasible ways to deal with typing:

1. Allow only a subset of types, for which typing is decidable, e.g., regular types [2] or even only mode annotations [15].
2. Require annotations where typing is not decidable without additional information.
3. Work on a best-effort basis which may let some type errors slip through.

Most type systems fall into the first or the second category. This usually limits expressiveness of the language: some efficient or idiomatic patterns may be rejected by the type system. As an example, most implementations of the Hindley-Milner type system [11] do not allow heterogeneous lists though always yield a well-typing of the program. Additionally, most type systems refuse to handle a proper "any" type when insufficient information is available and arguments may, statically, be any arbitrary value. Such restrictions render adaptation of type systems to existing projects infeasible. Annotations, however, can be used to guide type systems and allow more precise typing. The trade-off is code overhead introduced by the annotations themselves, which are often cumbersome to write and to maintain.

Into the last category falls the work of Schrijvers et al. [16], and, more well-known, the seminal work of Ciao Prolog [3] featuring a rich assertion language which can be used to describe types. Unfortunately, [16] seems to be abandoned after an early publication and the official release was removed. Ciao's approach, on the other hand, is very powerful, but suffers due to incompatibilities with other Prolog dialects.

We share the reasoning and philosophy behind Ciao's approach to typing [3]: type systems for languages such as Prolog must be optional in order to retain usefulness, power and expressiveness of the language even if it comes at the cost that not all type errors can be detected. Mycroft-O'Keefe identified two typical mistakes type systems uncover: firstly, omitted cases and, secondly, transposed arguments. We argue that omitted cases might as well be intended failure and, as such, cannot be uncovered in general. Thus, a type system should not be concerned with missing cases. Traditional type systems such as the seminal work of Mycroft-O'Keefe [12] often are not a good fit, as typing in Prolog is a curious case: due to backtracking and goal failure, type errors may lead to behaviour that is valid yet unintended.

Backtracking. Prolog predicates are allowed to offer multiple solutions which is often referred to as non-determinism. Once a goal fails, execution continues at the last choice point where another solution might be possible. Thus, if a predicate was called incorrectly, the program might still continue because another solution is found, e.g., based on other input. Consider an error in a specialised algorithm: if there is a choice point, a solution might still be found if another, slower, fall-back implementation is invoked via backtracking. Such errors could go unnoticed for a long time as they cannot be uncovered by testing if a correct solution is still found in a less efficient manner. In the example below, a sorting predicate tries to avoid the worst-case complexity of quick sort by checking whether the list is already sorted. Because an extra level of nesting is introduced on the tail when calling `sorted`, the call will backtrack into the second clause, execute a redundant sort operation and yield the correct result slower.

```
sort_list([H|T], [H|T]) :- sorted([H|[T]]), !. % type error, oop
sort_list(L, Sorted) :- qsort(L, Sorted).
```

Goal Failure. Most ISO Prolog predicates raise an error if they are called with incorrect types. However, non-ISO predicates usually fail as no solution is found because the input does not match with any clause. E.g., consider a predicate as trivial as `member`:

```
member(H, [H|_]). member(E, [_|T]) :- member(E, T).
```

Querying `member(1, [2,3,4])` will fail because *the first argument is not in the list*, which is the second argument. We name this *intended failure*. Yet, if the second argument is not a list, e.g., when called as `member(1, 2)`, it will fail because *the second argument is not a list*. We call this *unintended failure*, as the predicate is called *incorrectly*. The story gets even worse: additionally to failure cases, there can also be unintended *success*. Calling `member(2, [1, 2|foo])` is not intended to succeed, as the second argument is not a list, yet the query returns successfully. Distinguishing between intended and unintended behaviour is impossible as they use the same signal, i.e. goal failure (or success). We argue that the only proper behaviour would be to raise an error on unintended input instead because this most likely is a programming error.

In this paper, we investigate the following questions: Can we implement an optional type system that supports *any Prolog dialect*? How well does such a type system perform and is a subset of errors that are identified on *best-effort basis* sufficient? We think that the most relevant class of errors is that an argument is passed incorrectly, i.e. the type is wrong. Thus, an important question is how precise type inference by such a type system could be. If it works well enough, popular error classes such as transposed arguments (as described by [12]) can be identified in most cases.

3   Foundation: *plspec*

plspec is an ad-hoc type system that executes type checks at runtime via co-routining. With *plspec*, it is possible to add two kinds of annotations. The first kind of annotation allows introduction of new types. *plspec* offers three different ways for this: recombination of existing types, usage of a predicate that acts as characteristic function, and rules that check part of a term and generate new specifications for sub-terms. For our type system, we currently focus only on the first one and implement shipped special cases that fall under the third category, i.e. tuples, lists and compound terms.

plspec's built-in types are shown in Fig. 1. They correspond to Prolog types, with the addition of "exact", which only allows a single specified atom (like a zero-arity compound), and "any", which allows any value. Some types are polymorphic, e.g. lists can be instantiated as lists of a specific type. There are also two combinators: one_of (that allows union types) as well as and (which is the intersection of two types).

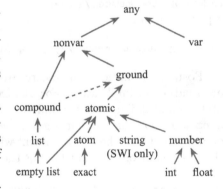

Fig. 1. Abstract type domain

Combination of built-in types is certainly very expressive. While such structures cannot be inferred easily without prior definition, as a realistic example, it is possible to define a tree of integer values by using the one_of combinator as follows:

```
defspec(tree, one_of([int, compound(node(tree, int, tree))])).
```

Valid trees are 1, node(1, 2, 3), node(node(0, 1, 2), 3, 4) but not, e.g. tree(1, 2, 3) (because the functor does not match) or node(a, b, c) (as it stores atoms instead of integer values). Note that it is also possible to use a wildcard type to define a tree `tree(specvar(X))`, which passes the variable down into its nodes. `specvars` are a placeholder to express that two or more terms share a common, but arbitrary type. This can be used to define template-like data structures, which can be instantiated as needed, e.g., as a `tree(int)`.

The second kind of annotations specifies how predicates may be called and, possibly, what parameters are return values. We re-use two different annotations for that: *Preconditions* specify types for all arguments of a predicate. For a call to be valid, at least one precondition has to be satisfied. *Postconditions* add promises for a predicate: if the predicate was called with certain types and if the call was successful, specified type information holds on exit. Pre- and postconditions must be valid for every clause of the specified predicate. Consider a variation of `member/2`, where the second argument *has to be* a list of atoms and the first argument can either be an `atom` or `var`:

```
atom_member(H,[H|_]).    atom_member(E,[_|T]) :- atom_member(E,T).
```

Instead of checking the terms in the predicate, type constraints describing intended input are added via *plspec*'s pre- and postconditions. The following preconditions express the valid types one has to provide: the first argument is either a variable or an atom and the second argument must be a list of atoms.

```
:- spec_pre(atom_member/2, [var, list(atom)]).
:- spec_pre(atom_member/2, [atom, list(atom)]).
```

As the second argument is always a ground list of atoms, we can assure callers of `atom_member/2` that the first term is bound after the execution using a postcondition:

```
:- spec_post(atom_member/2, [var, list(atom)], [atom, list(atom)]).
```

Postconditions for a predicate are defined using two argument lists: they are read as an implication. For `atom_member/2` above, this means that "if the first argument is a variable and the second argument is a list of atoms and if `atom_member/2` succeeds, it is guaranteed that the second argument is still a list of atoms and that the first argument will be bound to an atom". If the premise of the postcondition does not hold or the predicate fails, no information is gained.

Extensions to plspec. The traditional understanding of two instances of the same type variable, e.g., in a call such as `spec_pre(identity/2, [X, X])`, is that both arguments *share all types*. Yet, we want to allow heterogeneous lists and improve on the expressiveness of, say, `spec_pre(member/2, [X, list(X)])`. This extension is not yet implemented in *plspec* itself and is only part of the static analysis in *plstatic*. In order to express how the type of type variables is defined, we use `compatible` for the homogeneous and `union` for the heterogeneous case.

If a list is assigned the type `list(compatible(X))`, every item in the list is assigned the type `compatible(X)`. Then, *plstatic* checks whether all these terms share all types, thus enforcing a homogeneous list. If a list is assigned the type list(union(X)), every item in the list is assigned the type union(X). Instead of a type intersection, *plstatic* collects the types of these terms and builds a union type.

To give an example for the semantics of compatible and union, the list [1, a] has the *inner* type one_of([int, atom]) under the semantics of a union, and results in a type error (as the intersection of int and atom is empty) if its elements should be compatible. A correct annotation for member/2 would be the following postcondition:

spec_post(member/2,[any,list(any)],[compatible(X),list(union(X))]),

i.e., the list is heterogeneous, and the type of the first argument must occur in this list.

4   Our Type System

In the following, we describe a prototype named *plstatic*. It uses an abstract interpreter in order to collect type information on Prolog programs and additionally to identify type errors on a best-effort (based on available type information) basis, without additional annotations. The tool is available at https://github.com/isabelwingen/prolog-analyzer. Due to page limitation, we can only present some important parts of the tool.

Purpose and Result. The tool *plstatic* performs a type analysis on the provided code. All inferred information can be written out in form of annotations in *plspec* syntax or HTML data that may serve, e.g., as documentation. Naturally, *plstatic* shows an overview of type errors which were found during the analysis. We do not intend to uncover all possible type errors. Instead, we are willing to trade some false negatives for the absence of false positives, as they might overwhelm a developer in pure quantity. Whether true programming errors can be discovered is discussed in Sect. 5.

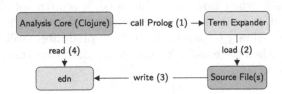

Fig. 2. Tool architecture

As typing can be seen as a special case of abstract interpretation [1], we use *plspec*'s annotations to derive an abstract value – a type – for terms in a Prolog clause. Abstract types correspond to the types shown in Fig. 1, where a type has an edge pointing to a strict supertype. However, as distinguishing ground from nonvar terms often is important, compound terms are tried to be abstracted to the ground type first, represented by the dashed edge. We use the least upper bound and greatest lower bound operations as they are induced by the type subset relation. This analysis is done statically and without concrete interpretation of Prolog code based on *plspec* annotations and term literals.

Annotations. plstatic works without additional annotations in the analysed code. It derives type information from (a large subset of) built-in (ISO) predicates, that we manually provided pre- and postconditions for. We also annotated a few popular libraries, e.g. the lists library. For predicates lacking annotations, types can be derived if type information exists for predicates called in their body, or can be inferred from unification with term structure in the code. Derived types describe intended success for the unannotated predicate. Naturally, precision of the type analysis improves with more annotations.

4.1   Tool Architecture

plstatic is implemented in Clojure. An alternative was to implement a meta-interpreter in Prolog. A JVM-based language allows easier integration into text editors, IDEs and potentially also web services. However, this requires to extract a representation of the Prolog program. We decided against parsing Prolog due to operator definitions and loss of term expansion (a mechanism that allows source-to-source transformation). Instead, we add a term expander ourselves before we load the program. It implements *plspec*'s syntax for annotations and extracts those alongside the program itself. All gathered information is transformed to edn (https://github.com/edn-format/edn).

plstatic consists of two parts pictured in Fig. 2: a binary (jar) that contains the static analysis core, and a term expander written in Prolog, The analysis core is started with parameters specifying the path to a Prolog source file or directory and a Prolog dialect (for now, "swipl" or "sicstus"). Additionally, the path to the term expander can be passed as an argument as well if another syntax for annotations than *plspec*'s is desired.

Regarding module resolution, special care has to be taken when an entire directory is analysed: when modules are included, it is often not obvious where a predicate is located. It can be hard to decide whether a predicate is user-defined, shipped as part of a library or part of the built-in predicates available in the user namespace. Thus, when the edn-file is imported, a data structure is kept in order to resolve calls correctly.

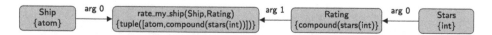

Fig. 3. An example environment (using edn-formatted maps)

As our evaluation in Sect. 5 uses untrusted third-party code, we take care that the Prolog code, that may immediately run when loaded, is not executed.

Instead, the term expander does not return any clause, effectively removing the entire program during compilation. Trusted term expanders can be loaded beforehand if required.

4.2 Analysis

Our approach to type inference implements a classical abstract interpreter. Each clause is analysed individually in a first phase. We use *plspec*'s annotations of the clause and the sub-goals to derive an abstract type for all occuring terms in a single clause. In a second phase, the results of several clauses are combined to a new postcondition, that may be more accurate than the one already provided. In this case, the analysis of a predicate would in turn improve the analysis result for clauses that call that predicate.

For this reason, *plstatic* works in two phases: first, clause-local analysis that is based on already known information, and second, merging information of all clauses of a single predicate, propagating newly gained information to the caller(s). Without the presence of a `one-of` combinator, this would guarantee a fixed point as a result of the analysis. As we cannot infer recursive datatypes yet, which might result in infinite `one-of`-sequences, we limit the number of steps in order to ensure termination.

Example: Rate My Ship The following code will accompany us during this section.

```
ship(Ship) :- member(Ship, [destiny, galactica, enterprise]).
rating(stars(Rate)) :- member(Rate, [1,2,3,4,5]).
rate_my_ship(S,R) :- ship(S), rating(R).
```

Preparation. For every loaded predicate, we check for existing pre- and post-conditions that are provided by the user or our own manual annotations of ISO predicates. Otherwise, they are created containing any-types during the preparation as follows: all literals (e.g., lists, compound or atomic terms) in the clause head are considered: their type is already known after loading the program. For variable literals, we initially assume an individual **any** type. Additionally, if not annotated otherwise, we assume that a clause may be called with variables. Based on this information, we create initial pre- and postconditions for all predicates, considering the *entire* argument vector.

Below, we show the generated specs for our example after the preparation step:

```
:- spec_pre(ship/1, [any]).
:- spec_post(ship/1, [any], [any]).
:- spec_pre(rating/1, [one_of([[var, compound([stars(any)])]])]).
:- spec_post(rating/1, [any], [compound([stars(any)])]).
:- spec_pre(rate_my_ship/2, [any, any]).
:- spec_post(rate_my_ship/2, [any, any], [any, any]).
```

Phase 1: Clause-Local Analysis. Because of the nondeterministic nature of Prolog, it is not sufficient to store the current type for a variable at a given point: we also have to consider relationships between several terms that are caused by unification. Such relationships are stored in an environment, for which we use a directed graph per clause. The inferred types of the terms are stored in the vertices. Relationships between terms and sub-terms as in [H|T], where head and tail might have a dependency on the entire list term (e.g., list(int)), or postconditions are saved as labelled edges between the term vertices. An example showing the structure of a compound term rate_my_ship(Ship,Rating) with some inferred types is given in Fig. 3.

During the analysis of a clause, the type domains of the terms are updated and their precision is improved. We assume that each predicate call in the body has to succeed and gather information from their pre- and postconditions. When new type information about a term is gained, the greatest lower bound is calculated by intersecting both domains. When considering variables in Prolog however, this comes with some pitfalls that are discussed in more details in *Step 2*. If the type intersection is empty, no concrete value is possible for the Prolog term and a type error is reported. However, this relies on the assumption that all given annotations are correct.

Step 1: Clause Head. The environment is initialised with all terms occurring in the head of the clause. Information about the head of the clause can be derived from the preconditions. According to *plspec*, at least one precondition must be fulfilled.

This raises the issue of tuple distributivity. Consider a predicate cake(X, Y) that is annotated with the preconditions [atom, int] and [int, atom]. This means that cake/2 expects an atom and an integer, no matter the order. For both X and Y, one could derive one_of([atom, int]) as type information. However, this would render X=1,Y=2 to be valid input, as the individual type constraints are fulfilled yet the original precondition is violated.

As we aim at keeping the most precise type information possible, we create an artificial tuple containing all arguments, whose domain is a union-type containing all supplied preconditions. This artificial term functions as a "watcher", and ensures all type constraints. For the cake predicate, the term [X,Y] is added to the environment, along with its type one_of([tuple([atom,int]), tuple([int,atom])]). Once we know a more specific type for, e.g., Y, we can derive which option must be valid for the "watcher", and we can derive a type for X. The environment is pictured in Fig. 4.

Due to page limitations, we only consider the environment of rate_my_ship/2 here: in this step, it infers types for S and R first, before combining dependencies between the variables in the entire argument vector [S,R].

Step 2: Evaluate Body. We analyse the body step by step, making use of (generated or annotated) pre- and postconditions of all encountered sub-goals. This allows us to refine the type step by step: for example, if rating(X) is called, one can infer that X must have the structure stars(_) on success, even if no information on the variable was known before. On the first occurrence of a term, it is added to the environment. Similarly to the clause head, at least one precondition of the sub-goal must be compatible with the combination of the arguments it is called with. Otherwise, if X is known not to be of the matching compound stars(_) but, e.g., an integer, a type error is raised.

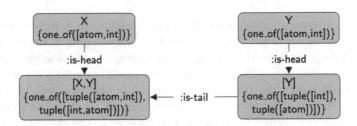

Fig. 4. Environment with a watcher (using edn-formatted maps)

Table 1. Environment for rate_my_ship/2

Variable term	Clause head	After 1st sub-goal	After 2nd sub-goal
[S, R]	tuple([any, any])	tuple([any, any])	tuple([any, any])
[R]	tuple([any])	tuple([any])	tuple([any])
R	any	any	compound(star([any]))
S	any	any	any

The analysis does not step into the sub-goal, and only uses pre- and postconditions. A postcondition specifies type constraints on a term after the called predicate succeeds. Thus, it is checked which premises of postconditions are fulfilled. Then, the greatest lower bound of the current type domain and the possible conclusion of the postconditions is calculated in order to improve precision. An example is shown in Table 1.

Type Variables. We have introduced two new kinds of type variables (cf. Sect. 3): union and compatible. It is possible to use union(X) or compatible(X), where X is a type variable. Both are placeholders for yet unknown types and express two different relationships between terms:

Every term that is assigned the type union(X) contributes to the definition of the type that is X. The connection is made by adding a labelled edge :union between the term and X. Then, the domain of all contributing terms is calculated as described. At the end of the analysis step, the union type of the variable X is inferred via the least upper bound of all connected terms. As an example, if an integer and an atom is part of the same union type, it will result in one_of(int, atom).

On the other hand, terms that are assigned the type `compatible(X)`, must be compatible with all other terms that are assigned that type. This implies that their intersection must not be empty. As with the `union` type, we create a labelled edge `:compatible` connecting the term to `X`. These edges are processed *after* all union edges have been visited. For example, if a known atomic value and a known integer have to be compatible within the same type variable, we can infer that both values have the type integer, as it is the intersection of both types.

In order to determine the type of a type variable, it is required to know all contributing terms. Thus, for compound or list terms of a known size, the assigned type is passed down to its sub-terms using the mechanisms described above. Yet, even if we know that `L` is a list of `union(X)`, we do not know the list items yet – even worse, the variable may only be bound later on! This requires an additional step in order to ensure that the domain for the type variable `X` is compiled correctly: we opted to add a `:has-type` edge to the environment, which connects a Prolog variable to an artificially created variable `T__<uuid>` storing the inner type, i.e. `union(X)` in the example above. Whenever the domain of a connected variable is updated, so is the type variable itself. Effectively, this delays the computation of the actual type variable. The artificial list type variable then is connected with `union(X)`. For `compound` and `tuple` *type specifications*, an artificial term is created and linked to the variable term via a special edge. This is required to mimic unification of Prolog variables. Whenever the domain of the variable term is updated, the artificial term's domain is updated as well. Finally, the information is propagated into the corresponding sub-terms if required.

Have a look at `member/2` used in the body of `ship/1`. The provided postcondition is

```
post_spec(member/2, [any, any], [compatible(X), list(union(X))]).
```

Therefore, after analysing the body of `ship/1`, we know the following:

1. The second argument of `member` contributes to the variable `X` in form of a *union*. We learn that `X` is either `destiny`, `galactica` or `enterprise`.
2. We learn that the variable `Ship` must be compatible with `X`, so it must be one of the three atoms named above.

Step 3: Term Relationships. After analysing the body, all terms in the clause are included in the environment. Then, nodes that may be destructured, i.e. lists and compound terms, are looked up in the graph. As sub-terms, e.g. `X` in `stars(X)`, can be used individually in subsequent sub-goals, i.e. without the wrapping functor `stars(_)`, inferred information has to be propagated back to the larger compound term. We introduce the following edges in order to provide the necessary mechanism: For lists, we extract the head and tail terms and add them to the environment if they are not already contained. Those terms are marked with special edges `:is-tail` and `:is-head` (cf. Fig. 4) pointing to the original list. For compounds, we add the argument terms to the environment and store the position of all sub-terms by adding an edge `:pos` (cf. Fig. 3).

For `rate_my_ship/2`, three edges are added due to this step: the environment already contains the argument vector `[S,R]` after *Step 1*. We add that `S` is the head item, that `[R]` is the tail of the list, and that `R` is the head of the tail `[R]`.

Prolog Variables. The any-type can be split into two disjoint sets: variables and non-variable terms. After processing a sub-goal, non-variable terms can only gain precision. Variables, however, have the unique property that their type can change, as they can be bound to, say, an atom, which is *not* a sub-type. To take this into account, a different intersection mechanism is required for variables:

– Preconditions of the *currently analysed* predicate may render a variable non-variable.
– Preconditions of a *called sub-goal* cannot render a variable term non-variable.
– Postconditions of a *called sub-goal* may render a variable term non-variable.
– Once a Prolog variable is bound to a non-variable, it behaves like any non-variable.

Step 4: Fixed-Point Algorithm. During the prior steps, we added edges to the environment. These are now used to update the types of the linked terms. If the environment no longer changes, we have consumed all collected knowledge and have found a preliminary result for a clause.

For example, in `rate_my_ship/2`, we will update the tuples `[R]` and `[S,R]` once we learn that `R` must be of the form `compound(stars([any]))`.

Phase 2: Global Propagation of Type Information. During the local analysis, each clause was inspected in isolation. The type domains in the returned environments contain the types after a successful execution of a clause *with the knowledge gained so far*. The gathered information then must be propagated to the caller of the corresponding predicate in order to improve the precision of the type inference.

Each resulting environment can be used to generate the conclusion of a post-condition. If a predicate succeeds, at least one of its clauses succeeded. As post-conditions must be valid for the entire predicate, the conclusion of a new post-condition is the union of all conclusions of the corresponding clauses. This newly gained knowledge (in form of a postcondition) is added to the analysed data for every predicate. Afterwards, both local analysis and global propagation are triggered until a fixed-point is reached. Inferred pre- and postconditions can be written out after analysis in *plspec*'s syntax.

Example: append/2. Consider the append program:

```
append([], Y, Y).     append([H|T], Y, [H|R]) :- append(T, Y, R).
```

For the first clause, *plstatic* would derive the types `[list(any), any, any]`. For the second clause, we gain no additional information from the body, because `append/2` is calling itself, so we derive the types [list(any), any, list(any)]. To create a conclusion of a postcondition for the predicate, we need to combine the results of the two clauses. Unfortunately, as the type of the third argument is any in one case, it swallows the more precise type list(any). We obtain the following conclusion: [list(any), any, any]. While the *intention* is that the second and third arguments are lists as well, this cannot be inferred without annotations.

As you have probably noticed, *plstatic* has not yet found the accurate type atom for S or R in rate_my_ship/2. This is because the pre- and postconditions of ship/1 have not been updated yet, so *plstatic* has no way of knowing that S is an atom. In the first phase, we have concluded that the argument given to ship/1 must be of type atom after a successful execution. As ship/1 has only one clause, we can infer the postcondition: :- post_spec(ship/1, [any], [atom]). Analogously, we obtain :- post_spec(rating/1, [any], [compound(stars([atom]))]).

The propagation of the newly gained knowledge is shown in Table 2. Afterwards we can update the pre- and postconditions for rate_my_ship/2, but ship/1 and rating/1 are not affected from this. If our program has no more clauses, the fixed-point is reached, and the analysis stops.

Table 2. Environment for rate_my_ship/2

Variable term	Newly gained knowledge	After propagation
[S, R]	tuple([any, compound(star([any]))])	tuple([*atom*, compound(star([*atom*]))])
[R]	tuple([compound(star([any]))])	tuple([compound(star([*atom*]))])
R	*compound(star([atom]))*	compound(star([atom]))
S	*atom*	atom

Backtracking. Preconditions specify a condition which must be fulfilled at the moment of the call, and postconditions can provide information about the type of the used terms after a successful execution. The caller of a predicate is unaware which clause provided the result. Thus, the union of all gained type information has to be considered in the second phase. As a result, it is safe to ignore backtracking: yet, precision could in some cases be improved if clause ordering and cuts (!) were considered.

5   Evaluation

To our knowledge, papers on type systems for Prolog usually omit an evaluation of their applicability for existing, real-world Prolog code and offer insights on their type inference mechanisms on small toy examples, such as the well-known append predicate. However, we want to consider code that is more involved than homework assignments. There is no indication to what extent type inference approaches are applicable to the real world, or how much work has to be spent re-writing code for full-fledged type systems.

In contrast, we baptise *plstatic* by fire and evaluate for how many variables in the code we can infer a type that is more precise than **any**. For this, we use smaller SWI community packages[1], as well as PROB [9], a model checker and constraint solver that currently consists of more than 120 000 lines of Prolog code.

5.1   Known Limitations

Currently, we face three limitations in *plstatic*: firstly, as we try to avoid widening whenever possible, i.e., we try to use the most precise type like a **one_of** instead of generalising to their common supertype, performance is not too good. Analysis of small projects runs neglectably fast, yet PROB requires several hours to complete a full analysis. Secondly, libraries throw a wrench into our scheme: modern Prolog systems pre-compile the code. Hence, meta-programs, such as term expanders, cannot access their clauses. Thus, library code is not considered and *plstatic* has to rely on annotations. Currently, we only provide annotations for large parts of the lists library (for both *SWI Prolog* and *SICStus Prolog*) and the AVL tree library (for *SICStus Prolog* only). Otherwise, for all library predicates that are not annotated, an **any** type has to be assumed. Thirdly, we currently do not consider disjunctions and if-then-else constructs, but may gain additional precision once this is implemented.

Additionally, there is an inherent limitation in our analysis strategy: some predicates may really work on *any* type, e.g. term type checking predicates (such as **ground/1** or **nonvar/1**) or the **member/2** predicate regarding the first argument. As no similar analysis for Prolog programs exists yet and type inference by hand is infeasible for large programs, it is certainly hard to gauge the precision of our type inference.

Table 3. Amount of Inferred Types for Variables

Repository	# Variables	Inferred types	Unknown calls
bddem	196	31.63%	57.6%
dia	400	68.5%	8.23%
maybe	32	6.25%	70.0%
plsmf	67	37.31%	37.5%
quickcheck	122	42.6%	34.1%
thousands	19	94.73%	0.0%
∅ SWI community packages	68344	21.8%	39.0%
PROB	81893	21.2%	20.8%

---

[1] http://www.swi-prolog.org/pack/list.

5.2 Empirical Evaluation

In Table 3, the results of some repositories[2] and the mean value of the 198 smallest community packages is shown. We give the amount of Prolog variables, and the percentage of which we can infer a type that is a strict sub-type of **any**. For reference, we also give the amount of calls to unknown predicates in order to give an idea how many missing types are caused by, e.g., library predicates lacking annotations. Though, once a variable is assigned an **any** type, the missing precision typically is passed on to terms that are interacting with the **any** term as the predicate is implemented in a library.

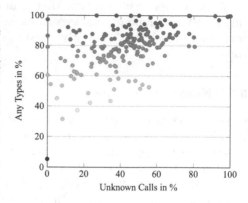

Fig. 5. Correlation between unknown calls and inferred types

At first glance, the fraction of inferred types seems to be rather low. For some repositories, such as "dia" and "thousands", a specific type could be inferred for a large percentage of variables. Note that in return, the amount of unknown calls is relatively low. Then, there are repositories such as "bddem" and "plsmf", which both are wrappers of a C library. As such, the interop predicates are unknown and the inferred types are significantly lower. Finally, there are packages like "maybe", "quickcheck" and projects such as PROB, that make use of other libraries, conditional compilation, meta-calls and other features that decrease accuracy of type inference.

Overall, we were surprised how small the amount of inferred types was. Though, one has to consider that a large amount of predicates are library calls, e.g. into the popular CLP and CHR libraries. In Fig. 5, we show this relation. One can clearly recognise that (unknown) library calls negatively impact the results of our type analysis. Yet, many auxiliary predicates are written to be polymorphic and deal with any type.

With *plstatic*, we were able to find several errors: many SWI libraries have been broken with changes introduced in *SWI Prolog* 7 [19]. Strings now are proper strings, where legacy code relies on the assumption that they are represented as code lists. Furthermore, *plstatic* located calls in PROB that were guaranteed to fail every time due to type errors. These calls decide whether a backend is usable in order to solve a given predicate and always fail. Thus, the errors have gone unnoticed for eight years, as the backend simply was not used. One error was reported due to missing term expansion as we did not execute untrusted Prolog code. We found another false-positive due to meta predicate annotations which add the module to a goal, thus altering the term structure. Additionally, we found some extensions *SICStus Prolog* made to the ISO

---

[2] Full results: https://github.com/pkoerner/plstatic-results/tree/wflp-20.

standard that we were not aware of: e.g., arithmetic expressions in *SICStus Prolog* allow expressions such as X is integer(3.14) or Y is log(2, 42). Thus, *plstatic* raised type errors for terms that did not match our type describing ISO arithmetic expressions.

6   Conclusion and Future Work

In this paper, we presented *plstatic*, a tool that re-uses its annotations in order to verify types statically where possible. In several existing Prolog repositories, *plstatic* was able to locate type errors. Yet, without annotations of further libraries, the amount of actual inferred types remains relatively low. We invite the Prolog community to discuss whether such type annotations are desired and should be shipped as part of packages. Such measures should be taken first in order to increase precision of the type inference before introducing run-time optimisations that, e.g., avoid exponential blow-ups. Then, it would be worthwhile to study the effects of such optimisations.

There remains some work on *plstatic*: performance bottlenecks need to be reviewed. Furthermore, the analysis would heavily benefit from a mechanism for the term expander to hook into library packages, manual annotations or generated annotations based on library source code as far as it is available. It might also be possible to analyse some pre-compiled library beforehand and re-use those results in the analysis of the main program. We also plan to implement semantics for new types, for which the structure is not specified, but they may only be created by libraries. E.g., Prolog streams cannot be created manually and one of the built-in predicates *must* be called. Other examples include ordered sets or AVL trees, where it is possible to create or manipulate such a term, but it is heavily discouraged as it is very easy to introduce subtle errors.

Moreover, it would be exciting to compare the amount of inferred types to similar implementations such as CiaoPP. We assume their analysis to be stronger, but suspect that Ciao's approach might not scale as well for larger programs. Yet, comparison might be hindered, again, because features of other Prolog systems are not supported. It might also be interesting to see whether our semantics can be integrated into CiaoPP.

In [18] and also in the evaluation of *plspec* [7], it was determined that the overhead of run-time type checks can be enormous, especially if applied to recursive predicates. With additional type information, a large amount of run-time checks can be eliminated, as, e.g., proposed by [18]. It is fairly straightforward to generate a list of already discharged annotations and use that as a blacklist in *plspec*. This could move the tool towards gradual typing [17], combining benefits of static typing and reducing overhead of checks at run-time with the potential for many optimisations.

It is well-known that compilers often benefit heavily from type information. An interesting research question is to investigate the impact of type information, e.g. gained by *plstatic* or by annotations, when added to the binding-time analysis of a partial evaluator, such as LOGEN [10]. This might greatly reduce the work required of manually improving generated annotations in order to gain additional performance.

As a more pragmatic approach to future work, it would be greatly appreciated if the state-of-the-art of Prolog development tooling could be improved. Currently, IDEs and editor integrations are lacking. Including type information would be a great start.

A   Formal Inference Rules

In the following, t denotes a Prolog term, and $t_1, \ldots, t_n$ its subterms. $A, B, A_1 \ldots A_n, B_1, \ldots, B_n$ denote types. We assume the existence of the following sets of types:

- The set $Ground$ containing all ground Prolog terms, i.e., all inputs for which the Prolog predicate `ground/1` returns true.
- The set Var containing all Prolog variables, i.e., all inputs for which the Prolog predicate `var/1` returns true.
- The set $List(A)$ that contains all (proper) Prolog lists containing only elements of type A. For example, $List(Int)$ contains the term `[1,2,3]`, but not the list `[a,b,c]`.
- The set $Compound(f(A_1, \ldots, A_n))$ containing all Prolog terms of the form $f(t_1, \ldots, t_n)$ with $t_1 \in A_1 \wedge \ldots \wedge t_n \in A_n$.
- The set $Tuple(A_1, \ldots, A_n)$ containing all Prolog lists of the form $[t_1, \ldots, t_n]$ with $t_1 \in A_1 \wedge \ldots \wedge t_n \in A_n$. In particular, this is shorthand notation for the type
  $Compound('.'(A_1, \ldots, Compound('.'(A_n, [])) \ldots)))$ and abstracts the concrete list constructor and terminator used in specific dialects of Prolog.
- The type $\perp$ contains no term and is used to indicate a type error.

Logic Foundations

$$\frac{t \in A \qquad t \in B}{t \in (A \cap B)} \qquad\qquad \frac{t \in A_1 \vee \ldots t \in \vee A_n \qquad t \in B}{t \in (A_1 \cap B) \vee \ldots \vee t \in (A_n \cap B)}$$

$$\frac{t \in A \vee t \in B \qquad A \subseteq B}{t \in A} \qquad\qquad \frac{t \in A \vee t \in B \qquad A \subseteq B}{t \in A}$$

Error Propagation

$$\frac{t \in List(\perp)}{t \in \perp}$$

$$\frac{t \in Tuple(A_1, \ldots, A_n) \qquad \exists 1 \leq k \leq n : A_k = \perp}{t \in \perp}$$

$$\frac{t \in Compound(f(A_1, \ldots, A_n)) \qquad \exists k, 1 \leq k \leq n : A_k = \perp}{t \in \perp}$$

$$\frac{t \in A_1 \vee \ldots \vee t \in A_n \qquad \exists 1 \leq k \leq n : A_k = \perp}{t \in A_1 \vee \ldots t \in A_{k-1} \vee t \in A_{k+1} \vee \ldots \vee t \in A_n}$$

Propagation of Ground in Compound Terms

$$\frac{t \in Compound(f(A_1, \ldots, A_n)) \qquad t \in Ground}{t \in Compound(f(A_1 \cap Ground, \ldots, A_n \cap Ground))}$$

$$\frac{t \in Tuple(A_1, \ldots, A_n) \qquad t \in Ground}{t \in Tuple(A_1 \cap Ground, \ldots, A_n \cap Ground)}$$

$$\frac{t \in List(A) \qquad t \in Ground}{t \in List(A \cap Ground)}$$

Intersection of Compound Terms

$$\frac{t \in Tuple(A_1, \ldots, A_n) \qquad t \in Tuple(b_1, \ldots, b_n)}{t \in Tuple(a_1 \cap b_1, \ldots, a_n \cap b_n)}$$

$$\frac{t \in Compound(f(A_1, \ldots, A_n)) \qquad t \in Compound(f(B_1, \ldots, B_n))}{t \in Compound(f(A_1 \cap B_1, \ldots, A_n \cap B_n))}$$

$$\frac{t \in List(A) \qquad t \in Tuple(A_1, \ldots, A_n)}{t \in Tuple(A_1 \cap A, \ldots, A_n \cap A)}$$

$$\frac{t \in List(A) \qquad t \in List(B)}{List(A \cap B)}$$

$$\frac{t \in Compound('.'(A_1, A_2)) \qquad t \in List(B)}{t \in List(B \cup A_1) \cup (A_2 \cap List(B))}$$

Special Case: Empty List

$$\frac{t \in List(A) \qquad t \in Atom}{t = []} \text{ not in SWI-Prolog} \qquad \frac{t \in Tuple()}{t = []}$$

$$\frac{t \in List(A) \qquad t \in Atomic}{t = []} \qquad \frac{t = []}{t \in List(A)} \forall \text{ types } A$$

Type Variables

$$\frac{t = [t_1, \ldots, t_n] \qquad t_1 \in A_1 \qquad \ldots \qquad t_n \in A_n}{t \in List(A_1 \cup \ldots \cup A_n)} \text{ when using union}$$

$$\frac{t = [t_1, \ldots, t_n] \qquad t_1 \in A_1 \qquad \ldots \qquad t_n \in A_n}{t \in List(A_1 \cap \ldots \cap A_n)} \text{ when using compatible}$$

$$\frac{t \in a_1 \vee \ldots \vee t \in a_n \qquad t \in B}{t \in (a_1 \cap B) \vee \ldots \vee t \in (a_n \cap B)}$$

Prolog Variables in Different Contexts

$$\frac{t \in Var \qquad t \in B \text{ is precondition} \qquad B \neq Var}{\perp}$$

$$\frac{t \in Var \qquad t \in B \text{ in clause head}}{B}$$

$$\frac{t \in Var \qquad t \in B \text{ is Postcondition}}{B}$$

References

1. Cousot, P.: Types as abstract interpretations. In: Proceedings POPL, pp. 316–331. ACM (1997)
2. Gallagher, J.P., Henriksen, K.S.: Abstract domains based on regular types. In: Demoen, B., Lifschitz, V. (eds.) ICLP 2004. LNCS, vol. 3132, pp. 27–42. Springer, Heidelberg (2004). https://doi.org/10.1007/978-3-540-27775-0_3
3. Hermenegildo, M.V., et al.: An overview of Ciao and its design philosophy. TPLP **12**(1–2), 219–252 (2012)
4. Jeffery, D.: Expressive type systems for logic programming languages. PhD thesis, Department of Computer Science and Software Engineering, The University of Melbourne (2002)
5. Jimenez, M., Lindahl, T., Sagonas, K.: A language for specifying type contracts in Erlang and its interaction with success typings. In: Proceedings ERLANG, pp. 11–17. ACM (2007)
6. Jones, S.P.: Haskell 98 Language and Libraries: The Revised Report. Cambridge University Press, Cambridge (2003)
7. Körner, P., Krings, S.: plspec – a specification language for prolog data. In: Seipel, D., Hanus, M., Abreu, S. (eds.) WFLP/WLP/INAP -2017. LNCS (LNAI), vol. 10997, pp. 198–213. Springer, Cham (2018). https://doi.org/10.1007/978-3-030-00801-7_13
8. Lakshman, T., Reddy, U.S.: Typed Prolog: a semantic reconstruction of the Mycroft-O'Keefe type system. In: ISLP, vol. 91, pp. 202–217 (1991)
9. Leuschel, M., Butler, M.: ProB: a model checker for B. In: Araki, K., Gnesi, S., Mandrioli, D. (eds.) FME 2003. LNCS, vol. 2805, pp. 855–874. Springer, Heidelberg (2003). https://doi.org/10.1007/978-3-540-45236-2_46
10. Leuschel, M., Craig, S.J., Bruynooghe, M., Vanhoof, W.: Specialising interpreters using offline partial deduction. In: Bruynooghe, M., Lau, K.-K. (eds.) Program Development in Computational Logic. LNCS, vol. 3049, pp. 340–375. Springer, Heidelberg (2004). https://doi.org/10.1007/978-3-540-25951-0_11
11. Milner, R.: A theory of type polymorphism in programming. J. Comput. Syst. Sci. **17**(3), 348–375 (1978)
12. Mycroft, A., O'Keefe, R.A.: A polymorphic type system for Prolog. Artif. Intell. **23**(3), 295–307 (1984)
13. Pfenning, F.: Types in Logic Programming. MIT Press Cambridge, Massachusetts (1992)
14. Pfenning, F.: On the undecidability of partial polymorphic type reconstruction. Fundam. Inform. **19**(1/2), 185–199 (1993)

15. Rohwedder, E., Pfenning, F.: Mode and termination checking for higher-order logic programs. In: Nielson, H.R. (ed.) ESOP 1996. LNCS, vol. 1058, pp. 296–310. Springer, Heidelberg (1996). https://doi.org/10.1007/3-540-61055-3_44

16. Schrijvers, T., Santos Costa, V., Wielemaker, J., Demoen, B.: Towards typed Prolog. In: Garcia de la Banda, M., Pontelli, E. (eds.) ICLP 2008. LNCS, vol. 5366, pp. 693–697. Springer, Heidelberg (2008). https://doi.org/10.1007/978-3-540-89982-2_59

17. Siek, J.G., Vitousek, M.M., Cimini, M., Boyland, J.T.: Refined criteria for gradual typing. In: Proceedings SNAPL. Schloss Dagstuhl-Leibniz-Zentrum fuer Informatik (2015)

18. Stulova, N., Morales, J.F., Hermenegildo, M.V.: Reducing the overhead of assertion run-time checks via static analysis. In: Proceedings PPDP, pp. 90–103. ACM (2016)

19. Wielemaker, J.: SWI-Prolog version 7 extensions. In: Proceedings CICLOPS-WLPE, p. 109 (2014)

Generating and Checking Exercises

A Framework for Generating Diverse Haskell-I/O Exercise Tasks

Oliver Westphal$^{(\boxtimes)}$

University of Duisburg-Essen, Duisburg, Germany
oliver.westphal@uni-due.de

Abstract. We present the design of a framework to describe parametrized exercise tasks on Haskell-I/O programming. Parametrized tasks can be instantiated randomly to quickly generate different instances of a task. Such automatic task generation is useful in many different ways. Manual task creation can be a time-consuming process, so formulating a task design once and then automatically generating different variations can save valuable time for the educator. The descriptions of tasks also serve as easy to understand documentation and can be reused in new task designs. On the student's side automatic task generation, together with an automated assessment system, enables practicing on as many fresh exercise tasks as needed. Students can also each be given a slightly different version of tasks, reducing issues regarding plagiarism arising naturally in an e-learning environment. Our task generation is centered around a specification language for I/O behavior we developed in earlier work. The task generation framework, an embedded domain specific language in Haskell, provides powerful primitives for the creation of various artifacts from specifications, including program code. We do not go into detail on the technical realization of these primitives. Our focus is on showcasing how such artifacts can be used as an alternative to the verbal description of requirements for different types of programming exercise tasks. By doing so, we are able to automatically generate a diverse range of task designs.

1 Introduction

We have recently designed and implemented a language for specifying console I/O programs [15,16] allowing us to formulate desired I/O behavior. The I/O behavior of programs, written in Haskell, can be tested probabilistically against specified behavior. We built this language to bring our testing capabilities of tasks on Haskell I/O more in line with how one can test tasks on pure programs, for example, using QuickCheck [1]. These automatic testing capabilities are used in the e-learning system [8,13] we use in our course on programming paradigms [9].

We now also aim to automatically generate the tasks themselves. This has a variety of advantages. Automatic task generation can help educators to create different variations of a common exercise task idea much quicker. When combined

© Springer Nature Switzerland AG 2021
M. Hanus and C. Sacerdoti Coen (Eds.): WFLP 2020, LNCS 12560, pp. 97–114, 2021.
https://doi.org/10.1007/978-3-030-75333-7_6

with automated assessment students have the opportunity to practice with as many fresh exercise tasks as they need. Automatically generated tasks can also be used to reduce plagiarism issues by giving students slight variations of the same task. We will (only) present automatic generation for tasks on Haskell I/O in this work, since our specification language is designed to describe the I/O behavior of programs. However, we believe our approach can be adapted for other types of exercise tasks as well.

Hand-written (programming) exercise tasks usually rely heavily on verbal descriptions. For example we might pose a task like this:

> *"Read a positive integer n from the console. Then, read n integers one after the other. Finally, output their sum."*

Such verbal descriptions are a big problem when trying to generate tasks automatically, as natural language generation is not exactly easy. Because of this, many task generation systems rely on templates defining a fixed (verbal) frame for a task. Such templates contain gaps to be filled to form a concrete task. Different (randomized) choices to fill these gaps result in different task variations. Depending on the domain for which tasks are generated, writing such a fixed framing, can be difficult. For example, it is easy for many different math tasks, where the verbal frame can be something like "Solve for x." together with a randomized equation. For programming tasks finding a fixed and general verbal frame is more difficult. Take, for example, the verbal description from above. We could use a fixed verbal skeleton like "First ... Then ... Finally" and fill it with random predefined descriptions. However, this is not a very flexible approach. Instead, our approach uses artifacts like program code or example runs of a program to achieve a fixed descriptions. Take, for example, the following task:

```
Give the programs interaction trace for input sequence 2, 4, 9.
prog :: IO ()
prog = do
  n ← readLn
  let loop s l =
    if l == n then print s
            else do
              v ← readLn
              loop (s + v) (l + 1)
  loop 0 0
```

The verbal description does not need to change, apart from maybe the given input sequence, no matter what we give as the program text. However, a solution to this task is fundamentally different than in the previous example. Instead of requiring a correctly behaving program, we simply ask for one specific run of a given program. Executing programs "by hand" is an important skill to have, but this task is not a substitute for a more open-ended programming task.

Our main contribution is to show that there is in fact a rich spectrum of different I/O tasks between these two extremes, as we will explore in Sect. 4.

Moving along this spectrum yields a diverse collection of tasks requiring different skills to solve. We design tasks ranging from program reading and comprehension over completion of partial programs all the way to writing original programs.

These designs are expressed in a newly developed Haskell embedded domain specific language (EDSL). This EDSL has two purposes. On the one hand it provides components to describe task designs and generate concrete task instances thereof. On the other hand, and equally important, it encourages descriptions that separate orthogonal aspects of task designs. This separation makes maintaining, expanding and reusing task designs much easier for the educator. Especially, when working with task designs created by another author, as it can also act as a form of documentation.

We build on top of the existing implementation of the specification language from our previous work. Starting from a specification, hand-written or generated randomly, we derive example runs and programs satisfying the specification. These artifacts are then used to build tasks. For example, we can give examples runs and ask for a corresponding program. Or we give a program and ask for runs of that program. The testing capabilities of the specification language allow us to automatically check solution candidates for such generated tasks for correctness.

We will not go into the technical details of how we create these artifacts in the implementation. Instead this presentation focuses on the framework's versatility in expressing interesting task ideas and generating variations.

We will first give a short overview of the previously introduced specification language. Next we will define the EDSL for describing tasks. Using both the specification language and the language of tasks together, we show how to design a diverse range of exercise tasks on Haskell-I/O.

2 Specifying and Testing I/O Behavior

Our previous work [15] introduced a specification language for I/O behavior. The goal of the language is to enable easy QuickCheck testing for I/O behavior. Specifications expressed in the language describe program behavior in terms of traces, i.e., sequences of read and written values, a program should produce. Programs are tested against specifications by repeatedly checking for different (carefully randomized) inputs whether the trace of that program matches the specification. We will not present a formal introduction of specifications as we did in our previous work [15]. A high-level overview of the language's features is enough for this work.

The language has typical elements of a standard imperative language, but varies in some aspects, most notably the use of variables. It defines primitives for reading and writing values from and to the console, a branching construct to choose sub-specifications based on Boolean conditions, and an iteration construct. Iteration is done through loops, but with explicit exit markers instead of a termination condition. Here is the summation behavior from the previous section expressed as a specification:

$$[\triangleright n]^{\mathbb{N}} ([\triangleright x]^{\mathbb{Z}} \angle len(x_A) = n_C \searrow \mathbf{E})^{\rightarrow \mathbf{E}} [sum(x_A) \triangleright]$$

Reading and writing, i.e., the primitive I/O action we want to observe, are written as $[\triangleright x]^{\tau}$ and $[t \triangleright]$, with x specifying the variable into which to read the value and t being a term describing the value to be written. Reading actions also have an annotation τ specifying the set of legal inputs we expect at that point. For example, we expect the first value read in the example specification to be a natural number. Branching on a Boolean condition c is written as $s_F \angle c \searrow s_T$, choosing the right branch s_T if c holds. Sub-specifications to be repeated are marked by $\to^{\mathbf{E}}$, and such a loop terminates on reaching an exit marker $\mathbf{E}$.

Variables in the specification language behave differently compared to classical imperative languages. They accumulate all values read into them. Variables are then either used as single values, i.e., the last value read into them, or as a list of all past values of that variable. The subscript of a variable indicates how it is used. C stands for the current value and A for all values. By design, specifications only define how inputs and outputs are interleaved and what the output values should be. They cannot describe internal states of a program.

The implementation, accompanying our previous work, exposes, besides constructors for Specifications, a simple API for testing programs against specifications. Testing relies on programs being expressed in a variant of the standard Haskell IO monad in which we can observe I/O effects [11,15]. This allows us to take a program, i.e., a value of the inspectable IO_{rep} type, and run it on an input sequence.

$$runProgram :: [\mathsf{String}] \to IO_{rep}\ () \to \mathsf{Trace}$$

We can then check whether the program run, encoded by its Trace of I/O actions, satisfies the behavior described by some Specification.

$$accept :: \mathsf{Specification} \to \mathsf{Trace} \to \mathsf{Bool}$$

Repeating this process for randomly generated input sequences, we formulate a QuickCheck Property stating that a program satisfies a specification.

$$fulfills :: IO_{rep}\ () \to \mathsf{Specification} \to \mathsf{Property}$$

We also provide an interpreter to turn specifications into executable programs.

$$buildComputation :: \mathsf{Specification} \to IO_{rep}\ ()$$

See [16] for details on this.

3   Describing Parameterized Tasks

This section introduces a small embedded domain specific language in Haskell to describe exercise tasks, including automatically checkable requirements. The language enables clear and concise descriptions of parameterized tasks. Descriptions can be built from orthogonal components allowing for quick and easy reuse and modification. We will use this language in Sect. 4 to discuss different categories of exercise tasks on Haskell I/O. The EDSL itself, however, can be used to describe parameterized tasks on any topic.

The language consists of three separate components. Descriptions of concrete exercise tasks, called task instances, a (sub-)language for describing requirements of correct solutions, and ways to express general task designs, i.e., generators for concrete tasks. Generally speaking, task designs bundle up generators for parameters together with a recipe for turning parameters into task instances.

The design goals of the EDSL are as follows:

- Clearly and concisely communicate the task's idea through its description, *without* exposing computational details or requiring knowledge thereof.
- Separate the basic building blocks of tasks into orthogonal and reusable components.
- The main purpose of a task's description is to be read by educators. Automatically checking whether a solution candidate fulfills a task's requirements is only a secondary feature.

First off we need a data type for concrete task instances.

```
data TaskInstance s = TaskInstance
  { question :: Description
  , given :: Maybe s
  , requires :: Require s }
```

The type parameter s represents the type of solution the TaskInstance expects. For simplicity we treat Description as an abstract string-like type for which we assume standard layout combinators exist [2]. Each TaskInstance can have a default *given* value of type s. By convention we treat this value as a somehow incomplete version of a correct solution to be used as a starting point for solving the task.

The Require type encodes the conditions under which a solution candidate is deemed correct. Requirements are not constructed directly, instead the EDSL provides constructor functions for different requirements. The simplest requirements are predicates on the solution type s.

```
requirePure :: (s → Bool) → Require s
```

For more complex requirements we use QuickCheck's Property type to enable randomized testing. QuickCheck also provides feedback in case the Property fails.

```
requireProp :: (s → Property) → Require s
```

We can also add an arbitrary IO pre-processing step to a requirement.

```
after :: Require s' → (s → IO (Maybe s')) → Require s
```

Maybe here indicates that pre-processing might fail, in which case the requirement is not fulfilled. One usage of this combinator, we will see later, is to compile programs given as textual input to actual Haskell values usable in a Property.

We define a primitive for building the conjunction of two requirements.

$(/\backslash)$ :: Require $s \rightarrow$ Require $s \rightarrow$ Require s

Lastly we might require a correct solution to "match" the *given* value of the TaskInstance. For example, filling in gaps in a given skeleton. We define a class to specify what matching a skeleton means for a specific type.

class Matches s **where**
    $matches :: s \rightarrow s \rightarrow$ Bool

Conceptually an instance of Matches defines a partial order on s where *matches* t s evaluates to True iff s is an extended version of the partial solution t.

$mustMatch ::$ Matches $s \Rightarrow s \rightarrow$ Require s
$mustMatch = requirePure \circ matches$

Checking whether a requirement holds for some value will in general require IO. Either to run QuickCheck or because we used *after*.

$check ::$ Require $s \rightarrow s \rightarrow$ IO Bool

Being able to represent concrete tasks, we can now define parameterized tasks as regular Haskell functions from parameters to TaskInstance values. For example, we can define a simple (non-I/O) task requiring adding up two numbers:

$taskAdd ::$ Int $\rightarrow$ Int $\rightarrow$ TaskInstance Int
$taskAdd\ x\ y =$ TaskInstance
    $\{\ question = text\ ($`"Give the sum of "` $+\!\!+\ show\ x\ +\!\!+$ `" and "` $+\!\!+\ show\ y)$
    $,\ given =$ Nothing
    $,\ requires = exactAnswer\ (x + y)\}$
$exactAnswer :: ($Eq $a,$ Show $a) \Rightarrow a \rightarrow$ Require a
$exactAnswer\ x = requireProp\ \$\ \lambda s \rightarrow s === x$

Defining *exactAnswer* in terms of QuickCheck's $(===)$ operator, we get informative feedback from QuickCheck's output in case of a test failure. Giving the wrong solution to an instance of the above task might, for example, result in the following error:

```
>check (requires (taskAdd 2 3)) 4
*** Failed! Falsified (after 1 test):
4 /= 5
```

The last step to automatic task generation is to couple a parameterized TaskInstance with a generator of its expected parameter.

data TaskDesign $s = \forall p.$TaskDesign
    $\{\ parameter ::$ Gen p
    $,\ instantiate :: p \rightarrow$ TaskInstance $s\}$

To instantiate a design we generate a parameter value and pass it to *instantiate*:

$generate TaskInstance$ :: TaskDesign s → IO (TaskInstance s)
$generate TaskInstance$ (TaskDesign *param inst*) =
    generate (*inst* <$> *param*)

We define combinators to aid in our goal of clearly communicating both a task's idea and requirements. Instead of using the TaskDesign constructor itself we use

for :: Gen p → (p → TaskInstance s) → TaskDesign s
for = TaskDesign

resulting in the general pattern

some Task :: TaskDesign s
some Task = *for someRandomParameter doSomething*
    where *someRandomPrameter* :: Gen p
        doSomthing :: p → TaskInstance s

The arguments to *for* are deliberately named to make the expression read like a high-level description of the task.

Generators can be combined and modified by specialized instantiations of well known combinators on monads and arrows [3]. The new names of these combinators reflect their domain specific usage and thereby aid in hiding computational details from task descriptions. The first of these combinators is

fixed :: p → Gen p
fixed = *pure*

allowing us to write *for* (*fixed parameter*) *doSomething* when we do not want to generate randomized tasks but still use the EDSL to communicate our design. Next we define

from :: (a → Gen b) → Gen a → Gen b
from = (=≪)

so that we can describe parameter generators in terms of existing generators:

for (*randomParameterB* 'from' *randomParameterA*) *doSomething*

Splitting up parameter generators separates different layers of randomness. Each layer can then easily be changed independently. For example, we can change *randomParameterA* to a fixed example

for (*randomParameterB* 'from' *fixed a*) *doSomething*

while *randomParameterB* is untouched. The parameter used to create a task instance is still randomized, but with one layer of randomness less.

The *instantiate* function can only ever take a single argument. For tasks with multiple randomized parameters we define combinators for tuple generators.

$$(\&\&\&\&) :: \mathsf{Monad}\ m \Rightarrow (a \rightarrow m\ b) \rightarrow (a \rightarrow m\ b') \rightarrow a \rightarrow m\ (b, b')$$
$$(****) :: \mathsf{Monad}\ m \Rightarrow (a \rightarrow m\ b) \rightarrow (a' \rightarrow m\ b') \rightarrow (a, a') \rightarrow m\ (b, b')$$

Looking ahead to Sect. 4, here is an example of how these combinators can be used to describe a TaskDesign.

> *for*
>   ((*exampleTrace* &&&& *haskellProgram*) '*from*' *randomSpecification*)
>   *giveInteractionTrace*

The names of the individual components and the usage of the combinators clearly communicate the basic idea of this TaskDesign. The expression reads almost like actual instructions for a task. This makes it easy for someone familiar with the EDSL, like a teaching assistant, to quickly modify and reuse parts of the design.

4   Building Tasks on Haskell I/O

With a general mechanism for describing tasks in place, we will now build some actual tasks on Haskell I/O programming. The source code of the implementation and all examples from this paper, can be found at https://github.com/fmidue/IOTasks.[1] First we introduce an alias for the type of inspectable I/O computations (see Sect. 2) to clearly separate it from syntactic program text.

> **type** ExecutableHaskell $= IO_{rep}\ ()$

Our example tasks do not expect ExecutableHaskell as solution candidates but instead use syntactic HaskellCode. For brevity we keep HaskellCode abstract here. It is enough to know that we can inspect and print out values of this type.

Using *fulfills* from Sect. 2 we can construct our first I/O specific requirement for a correct task solution.

> *mustSatisfy* :: Specification $\rightarrow$ Require ExecutableHaskell
> *mustSatisfy* $s = requireProp$ ('*fulfills*'s)

In order to be able to also check requirements like *mustSatisfy* we provide a function

> *compile* :: HaskellCode $\rightarrow$ IO (Maybe ExecutableHaskell)

to obtain semantic programs from syntactic representations. Together with *after* we can now build semantic requirements for syntactic programs. For example,

---

[1] The repository also contains instructions explaining how to generate and inspect random task instances, for the given examples.

```
passesCompiler :: Require HaskellCode
passesCompiler = requirePure (const True) `after` compile
```

requires program text to be valid Haskell. We will define additional requirements as we discuss the various example tasks.[2]

As hinted at earlier, we cannot rely only on verbal descriptions to convey a task's requirements. Instead we will use fixed verbal instructions in combination with program code and/or interaction traces. Our framework provides generators to build programs satisfying a given specification.

```
haskellProgram :: Specification → Gen HaskellCode
pythonProgram :: Specification → Gen PythonCode
```

We use randomized generators to create program code from specifications as there usually are different ways to implement the given behavior. Having access to different programs for the same specification is also useful for certain types of task designs, as we will see later on. For program code we mainly use Haskell code in our tasks, but it is also useful to have access to code in other languages and paradigms. For example, we use Python code to highlight how I/O looks different in Haskell compared to an imperative language. Our students should already know Python as it is taught in their introductory programming course.

We will not discuss the full details of this code generation. Our focus is on showcasing the different types of tasks expressible by the framework.

Essentially the code generation translates a given specification into an abstract program representation, agnostic about implementation techniques. These programs can be translated to a concrete language's syntax, like Haskell or Python, by choosing appropriate embeddings of iteration, branching, state passing, etc. Rewriting the intermediate representation, using predefined rules, we obtain slightly different programs for the same specification. This approach also allows us to generate programs with (randomized) gaps or programs containing certain syntactic errors and anti-patterns.

The framework also provides generators for example traces matching a specification.

```
exampleTrace :: Specification → Gen Trace
exampleTraces :: Int → Specification → Gen [Trace]
```

Since all of the artifact generators require specifications as parameters, suitable generators are assumed to exist. These generators are meant to be implemented by an educator/user as it is difficult to provide good generic generators. A sketch of how to write generators for specifications can be found in [16]. For our purposes we assume to have two generators:

```
randomSpecification :: Gen Specification
similarSpecifications :: Gen (Specification, Specification)
```

---

[2] All code shown in this section is part of the framework's API, except for expressions of type $p →$ TaskInstance s and TaskDesign s. Values of these two types should be read as defined by the framework's user.

The first generates a sensible random specification, for the educator's (task-specific) definition of sensible. The second generates a pair of similar looking specifications with differing behavior. Differing specification, for example, might have slightly different loop-termination conditions or varying outputs.

With all of these tools we now describe a diverse range of task designs. Following Le and Pinkwart [6] we classify these tasks into three classes:

1) Tasks with a single correct answer
2) Tasks with multiple correct answers but only a single solution strategy
3) Tasks with multiple different solution strategies

In our case these classes correspond to the complexity of requirement descriptions and roughly to task difficulty. Our introductory examples for programming tasks from Sect. 1 sit at the two extreme points of this class spectrum. The task with only a verbal description and no restrictions on the programming techniques to use is a perfect example of a class 3 task. Adding additional requirements to such a task moves it further towards or into class 2. On the other side of the spectrum, asking for a given program's behavior on a specific input is a class 1 task. The rest of this section will explore different points on this spectrum. Starting with class 1 tasks, we try to get as close to verbal-only free form tasks as possible. Pedagogically, this spectrum can also be seen as a progression of consecutive exercise tasks, developing students abilities to read, reason about, expand and finally write programs [12].

4.1   Tasks with One Correct Answer

Tasks with only a single correct answer cannot require a student to do any "real" programming. Even for small programs there is almost never only one right answer. Class 1 tasks are usually quiz-like tasks that focus on program reading and comprehension or simple program completion.

The simplest option to build such a task from our I/O related primitives is giving students two (or more) artifacts and asking them whether these artifacts originated from the same specification. For example, given two programs, determine whether they have the same behavior.

```
data BinDesc = Yes | No deriving (Eq, Ord, Enum, Show)
decision :: TaskDesign BinDesc
decision = for (equalityProblem 'from' similarSpecifications) checkAgreement
checkAgreement :: (BinDesc, HaskellCode, HaskellCode) → TaskInstance BinDesc
checkAgreement (haveSameBehavior, p_1, p_2) = TaskInstance
    { question = text "Do these two programs have the same behavior?"
      $$ text (show p_1) $$ text "---" $$ text (show p_2)
    , given = Nothing
    , requires = exactAnswer haveSameBehavior }
```

For simplicity we assume that there are at least two different programs for each specification.

$$equalityProblem :: (\mathsf{Specification}, \mathsf{Specification})$$
$$\rightarrow \mathsf{Gen}\ (\mathsf{BinDesc}, \mathsf{HaskellCode}, \mathsf{HaskellCode})$$
$$equalityProblem\ (s_1, s_2) = \mathbf{do}$$
$$\quad sameBehavior \leftarrow elements\ [\mathsf{No}, \mathsf{Yes}]$$
$$\quad (p_1, p_2) \leftarrow \mathbf{if}\ sameBehavior == \mathsf{Yes}$$
$$\quad\quad \mathbf{then}\ differentPrograms\ s_1\ s_1$$
$$\quad\quad \mathbf{else}\ differentPrograms\ s_1\ s_2$$
$$\quad pure\ (sameBehavior, p_1, p_2)$$

$$differentPrograms :: \mathsf{Specification} \rightarrow \mathsf{Specification}$$
$$\rightarrow \mathsf{Gen}\ (\mathsf{HaskellCode}, \mathsf{HaskellCode})$$
$$differentPrograms\ s_1\ s_2 = \mathbf{do}$$
$$\quad p_1 \leftarrow haskellProgram\ s_1$$
$$\quad p_2 \leftarrow haskellProgram\ s_2\ `suchThat`\ (/= p_1)$$
$$\quad return\ (p_1, p_2)$$

To illustrate what instances of the *decision*-task from above can look like here is an example of two similar looking programs with slightly different behavior. The second program is obtained by modifying the specification underlying the first program, in this case the loop-termination condition was randomly changed and the no longer needed initial input deleted.

```
p₁ = do                           p₂ = do
  n ← readLn                        let loop xs acc =
  let loop xs =                       if acc == 5
    if length xs == n                 then do print xs
      then do return xs               else do
      else do                           v ← readLn
        v ← readLn                       loop (xs + v) (acc + 1)
        loop (xs ++ [v])          loop 0 0
  ys ← loop []
  print (sum ys)
```

Tasks on program completion use the possibility to generate partial programs we hinted at in Sect. 3. We use a generator

$$haskellWithGaps :: \mathsf{Specification} \rightarrow \mathsf{Gen}\ \mathsf{HaskellCode}$$

that produces an I/O program with gaps. These gaps need to be filled with either *readLn* or *print*. The different types of these two functions ensure there is only one correct solution. For such a program we require choosing an appropriate expression for each gap.

```
completion1 :: TaskDesign HaskellCode
completion1 = for (haskellWithGaps 'from' randomSpecification) fillGaps
fillGaps :: HaskellCode → TaskInstance HaskellCode
fillGaps skeleton = TaskInstance
  { question = text "Complete the following program."
    $$ text "(Replace ? with readLn or print)"
  , given = Just skeleton
  , requires = passesCompiler /\ mustMatch skeleton }
```

For the last type of answer, traces, we can give a Haskell program and some input sequence and ask students to execute the program on that input. Fixing the input sequence, there is only one correct solution to such a task.

```
comprehension₁ :: TaskDesign Trace
comprehension₁ = for
  ((exampleTrace &&&& haskellProgram) 'from' randomSpecification)
  giveInteractionTrace
giveInteractionTrace :: (Trace, HaskellCode) → TaskInstance Trace
giveInteractionTrace (t, prog) = TaskInstance
  { question = text ("Give the program's trace for input sequence")
    <> text (show (inputs t))
    $$ text (show prog)
  , given = Nothing
  , requires = exactAnswer t }
inputs :: Trace → [String]
```

This design can, for example, generate the task from page 2.

4.2 Tasks with Multiple Correct Answers

Before moving on to tasks on actual programming, we first look at a class 2 variant of the last task from the previous section. Instead of giving a fixed input sequence we ask for an interaction trace with a certain property. One possibility is to give two similar looking programs with different semantics and ask for an input sequence for which the given programs exhibit different I/O behavior.

$comprehension_2$ :: TaskDesign [String]
$comprehension_2 = for$
  (($specificationAnd$ $haskellProgram$ **** $specificationAnd$ $haskellProgram$)
    'from' $similarSpecifications$)
  $findDiffSequence$

$findDiffSequence$ :: ((Specification, HaskellCode), (Specification, HaskellCode))
                $\rightarrow$ TaskInstance [String]
$findDiffSequence$ $((s_1, p_1), (s_2, p_2))$ = TaskInstance
  { $question$ = $text$ "Find inputs resulting in different behavior."
    $$ $text$ ($show$ p_1) $$ $text$ "---" $$ $text$ ($show$ p_2)
  , $given$ = Nothing
  , $requires$ = $triggerDifference$ s_1 s_2 }

$triggerDifference$ :: Specification $\rightarrow$ Specification $\rightarrow$ Require [String]
$triggerDifference$ s_1 s_2 = $requireProp$ $ $\lambda is \rightarrow$
  $((=\!/\!=)$ 'on' ($runProgram$ is $\circ$ $buildComputation$)) s_1 s_2

$specificationAnd$ :: (Specification $\rightarrow$ Gen a) $\rightarrow$ Specification
            $\rightarrow$ Gen (Specification, a)
$specificationAnd$ g = $pure$ &&&& g

The requirement uses the *buildComputation* function shown in Sect. 2 to derive executable programs from the specifications. Executing the specifications this way is easier than executing the displayed programs since these only exist in a textual form.

So far, our tasks are straightforward with regard to the questions asked. For programming tasks beyond gap filling we now need to describe the required behavior of programs as well as restrict which solution strategies are valid. To start off, we give interaction traces, i.e., example runs, to specify behavior and fix a solution strategy by providing a skeleton to complete.

```
completion₂ :: TaskDesign HaskellCode
completion₂ = for
  (exampleTraces 5 'from' fixed specification)
  matchExamples
  where specification = ...

matchExamples :: [Trace] → TaskInstance HaskellCode
matchExamples ts = TaskInstance
  { question = text "Complete the program to match the examples:"
      $$ vcat (map (text ∘ show) ts)
  , given = Just skeleton
  , requires = produceTraces ts 'after' compile /\ mustMatch skeleton }
  where skeleton = fromSourceString $ unlines
    ["main = do"
    ,"    ?"
    ,"  while ? ? ?"
    ,"while :: (a -> Bool) -> (a -> IO a) -> a -> IO a"
    ,"while = ..."]

produceTraces :: [Trace] → Require ExecutableHaskell
produceTraces ts = requirePure $ λp →
  all (λt → runProgram (inputs t) p == t) ts

fromSourceString :: String → HaskellCode
```

This task asks to produce the given examples by mimicking an imperative loop using the higher-order *while* function. For simplicity we use a fixed specification instead of a random one. Using a random specification, without any further restrictions, potentially results in an unsolvable task since the skeleton can have the wrong structure for the underlying behavior. With a suitable generator, however, the underlying specification can be randomized as well.

Using traces to describe behavior requirements has a disadvantage one needs to be aware of. Such descriptions may not fully characterize the underlying specification's behavior. The description essentially gives a list of unit tests for a solution to fulfill. The underlying specification guarantees there is at least one program solving the task without hard-coding the given examples. However, a program working only for the given examples and crashing on all others inputs still meets the requirement. In the above task such solutions are largely ruled out by the skeleton. For free-form programming tasks that do not use a skeleton, this is a more serious problem. Our solution is to use program code itself to describe the required behavior. Doing so naturally gives rise to two exercise types: refactoring and cross-language re-implementation.

Refactoring tasks ask to rewrite a given program into a program that satisfies certain properties the original program does not have. Both programs should behave identically, with regards to I/O, for the same inputs. The original program therefore fully describes the behavior a correct solution should have.

The next example gives a program accumulating list values and outputting the result of a computation, expressible as a fold, on this list. Students are asked to rewrite this program into a version not using any list, directly carrying out the computation.

> *refactoring* :: TaskDesign HaskellCode
> *refactoring* = *for*
>   (*specificationAnd haskellFoldProgram* 'from' *fixed specification*)
>   *rewriteToNoLists*
>   **where** *specification* = *undefined*
> *rewriteToNoLists* :: (Specification, Description) → TaskInstance HaskellCode
> *rewriteToNoLists* (*spec, prog*) = TaskInstance
>   { *question* =
>   *text* "Re-write the program such that it does not use lists."
> $$ *prog*
>   , *given* = Nothing
>   , *requires* = (*mustSatisfy spec* 'after' *compile*) /\ *noLists* }
> *noLists* :: Require HaskellCode
> *noLists* = *requirePure* $ λp →
>   *not* (*containsFunction* "++" p ∨ *containsFunction* ":" p)
> *containsFunction* :: String → HaskellCode → Bool
> *haskellFoldProgram* :: Specification → Gen Description

We check the requirement of not using lists by simply verifying that solution code does not contain the functions to build lists. Once again, the exact details on how *haskellFoldProgram* is implemented internally are outside the scope of this presentation. We basically take a program and look for a function known to be a fold, e.g. *sum* or *length*, that is used on the result of a list accumulating loop. This function's base case and recursive step are then "inlined" into the loop.

4.3 Tasks with Different Solution Strategies

For our last example we finally arrive at a task very similar to the verbal-only free-form tasks from the beginning. The task requires re-implementing a Python program in Haskell. As already stated above, we choose Python since our students learn it as their first programming language and are therefore already familiar with it.

$pythonToHaskell$ :: TaskDesign HaskellCode
$pythonToHaskell = for$
  ($specificationAnd\ pythonProgram$ 'from' $randomSpecification$)
  $rewriteAsHaskell$

$rewriteAsHaskell$ :: (Specification, PythonCode) $\rightarrow$ TaskInstance HaskellCode
$rewriteAsHaskell\ (s, prog) =$ TaskInstance
  { $question = text$ `"Write the following program in Haskell:"`
    $$ $text\ (show\ prog)$
  , $given =$ Nothing
  , $requires = mustSatisfy\ s$ 'after' $compile$ }

This task does not fix a solution strategy. By starting from a Python program it precisely states the required behavior. The Python program also does not contain any information on how a Haskell program with the identical behavior could look like. I/O programs in Haskell usually have a different structure compared to imperative languages (e.g. recursive functions vs. explicit loops). Take, for example, the following task instance generated from the above design.

```
Re-implement the following Python program in Haskell:
n = int(input())
x = []
while len(x) != n :
  v = int(input())
  x += [v]
print(sum(x))
```

The required behavior is the same as the verbal description from the introduction. It is clear that we need to use some form of repetition in our solution, but that information is also contained in the verbal description (*"read n integers one after the other"*). Only the usage of a list to store read integers is not in the verbal description. For everyone with basic programming skills this should not be anything new. We therefore argue that the above Python program can replace the verbal description without loosing precision or providing additional hints.

5   Related Work

Tools for automatic task generation exist in a variety of different application areas, for example, general science questions [14], math related tasks [5] and programming tasks [7,10]. Some systems for natural language questions can generate tasks from databases of domain specific text [14], but most approaches use templates together with parameter generators, similar to our TaskDesigns. In contrast to our flexible EDSL approach most of these systems use rigid template formats provided as inputs to the task generation. Consequently, these systems are usually embedded inside a specific e-learning environment. Our framework can, in principle, be used with any e-learning system. We already use a modular e-learning system [8,13] and plan to integrate the framework in that context.

Our generated task instances do not provide any detailed feedback apart from maybe some QuickCheck outputs. There are other automatic assessment systems providing more detailed feedback, including suggestions on how to fix mistakes. A survey of different automatic assessment systems for programming tasks and the feedback they can generate is presented by Keuning et al. [4].

6   Conclusion and Future Work

The presented framework can be used to describe a diverse range of exercise task designs and generate concrete randomized instances from these designs. Separating task descriptions into orthogonal components makes modifying and reusing tasks easy. Task designs also serve as high-level documentation for the task's idea if we choose descriptive names for the individual components.

We presented examples of using the framework to describe tasks on Haskell I/O. The variety in these tasks stems from domain specific primitives providing different artifacts around which the parameterized tasks are built. These artifacts are used as stand-ins for verbal descriptions to precisely state task requirements even if tasks are built from randomized specifications. Tasks created this way have a slightly different feel compared to traditional hand-written ones. Even though there are some restrictions to our approach, we can still create a wide range of different task types. To the best of our knowledge automatically deriving artifacts for communicating requirements is a novel approach to automatic task generation in the context of programming tasks.

We have not yet had the opportunity to use tasks like the ones shown in Sect. 4 in practice. However, our tasks on Haskell I/O-programming already use the specification language and its testing facilities. We plan to test the presented approach to task design in the next iteration of our programming paradigms course. We are especially interested to see whether tasks on program completion and comprehension benefit students when learning Haskell-I/O. Writing high-quality generators for specifications should also be investigated further. Good generators have a big influence on the quality of concrete task instances.

References

1. Claessen, K., Hughes, J.: QuickCheck: a lightweight tool for random testing of Haskell programs. In: Proceedings of the International Conference on Functional Programming, pp. 268–279. ACM (2000). https://doi.org/10.1145/351240.351266
2. Hughes, J.: The design of a pretty-printing library. In: Jeuring, J., Meijer, E. (eds.) AFP 1995. LNCS, vol. 925, pp. 53–96. Springer, Heidelberg (1995). https://doi.org/10.1007/3-540-59451-5_3
3. Hughes, J.: Generalising monads to arrows. Sci. Comput. Program. 37(1–3), 67–111 (2000). https://doi.org/10.1016/S0167-6423(99)00023-4
4. Keuning, H., Jeuring, J., Heeren, B.: A systematic literature review of automated feedback generation for programming exercises. ACM Trans. Comput. Educ. 19(1), 3:1–3:43 (2019). https://doi.org/10.1145/3231711

5. Kurt-Karaoglu, F., Schwinning, N., Striewe, M., Zurmaar, B., Goedicke, M.: A framework for generic exercises with mathematical content. In: International Conference on Learning and Teaching in Computing and Engineering, LaTiCE 2015, pp. 70–75. IEEE (2015). https://doi.org/10.1109/LaTiCE.2015.11

6. Le, N.T., Pinkwart, N.: Towards a classification for programming exercises. In: Proceedings of the 2nd Workshop on AI-Supported Education for Computer Science, AIEDCS 2014 (2014)

7. Mosbeck, M., Hauer, D., Jantsch, A.: VELS: VHDL e-learning system for automatic generation and evaluation of per-student randomized assignments. In: IEEE Nordic Circuits and Systems Conference, NORCAS 2018: NORCHIP and International Symposium of System-on-Chip (SoC), pp. 1–7. IEEE (2018). https://doi.org/10.1109/NORCHIP.2018.8573455

8. Rahn, M., Richter, A., Waldmann, J.: The Leipzig autotool e-learning/e-testing system. In: Symposium on Math Tutoring, Tools and Feedback. Open Universiteit Nederland (2008). http://www.imn.htwk-leipzig.de/~waldmann/talk/08/ou08/tool.pdf. Accessed July 2020

9. Siegburg, M., Voigtländer, J., Westphal, O.: Automatische Bewertung von Haskell-Programmieraufgaben. In: Proceedings of the Fourth Workshop "Automatische Bewertung von Programmieraufgaben", pp. 19–26. GI (2019). https://doi.org/10.18420/abp2019-3

10. Striewe, M., Balz, M., Goedicke, M.: A flexible and modular software architecture for computer aided assessments and automated marking. In: CSEDU 2009 - Proceedings of the First International Conference on Computer Supported Education, Lisboa, Portugal, 23–26 March 2009, vol. 2, pp. 54–61. INSTICC Press (2009)

11. Swierstra, W., Altenkirch, T.: Beauty in the Beast. A Functional Semantics for the Awkward Squad. In: Proceedings of the Haskell Workshop, pp. 25–36. ACM (2007). https://doi.org/10.1145/1291201.1291206

12. Van Merriënboer, J.J.G., De Croock, M.B.M.: Strategies for computer-based programming instruction: program completion vs. program generation. J. Educ. Comput. Res. **8**(3), 365–394 (1992). https://doi.org/10.2190/MJDX-9PP4-KFMT-09PM

13. Waldmann, J.: Automatische Erzeugung und Bewertung von Aufgaben zu Algorithmen und Datenstrukturen. In: Proceedings of the ABP, CEUR WS, vol. 2015 (2017)

14. Welbl, J., Liu, N.F., Gardner, M.: Crowdsourcing multiple choice science questions. In: Proceedings of the 3rd Workshop on Noisy User-Generated Text, NUT@EMNLP 2017, pp. 94–106. Association for Computational Linguistics (2017). https://doi.org/10.18653/v1/w17-4413

15. Westphal, O., Voigtländer, J.: Describing Console I/O Behavior for Testing Student Submissions in Haskell. In: Proceedings of the Eighth and Ninth International Workshop on Trends in Functional Programming in Education, EPTCS, vol. 321, pp. 19–36. EPTCS (2020). https://doi.org/10.4204/EPTCS.321.2

16. Westphal, O., Voigtländer, J.: Implementing, and Keeping in Check, a DSL Used in E-learning. In: Nakano, K., Sagonas, K. (eds.) FLOPS 2020. LNCS, vol. 12073, pp. 179–197. Springer, Cham (2020). https://doi.org/10.1007/978-3-030-59025-3_11

Constraint Programming

Formally Verified Transformation of Non-binary Constraints into Binary Constraints

Catherine Dubois[(✉)][iD]

ENSIIE, Samovar, Évry-Courcouronnes, France
catherine.dubois@ensiie.fr

Abstract. It is well known in the Constraint Programming community that any non-binary constraint satisfaction problem (with finite domains) can be transformed into an equivalent binary one. One of the most well-known translations is the Hidden Variable Encoding. In this paper we formalize this encoding in the proof assistant Coq and prove that any solution of the binary constraint satisfaction problem makes it possible to build a solution of the original problem and vice-versa. This formal development is used to complete the formally verified constraint solver developed in Coq by Carlier, Dubois and Gotlieb in 2012, making it a tool able to solve any n-ary constraint satisfaction problem, The key of success of the connection between the translator and the Coq binary solver is the genericity of the latter.

1 Introduction

Constraint Programming (CP) or Constraint Satisfaction Problems [14] have many real-life applications such as decision making, resource allocation, scheduling, vehicle routing, configuration, planning, program verification, etc. In this paradigm, models are made of variables, domains which define the possible values of the variables and constraints which restrict the space of solutions. For example, modeling a Sudoku game requires $9 * 9$ variables representing the different cells, their domain is the interval 1..9 and the constraints impose that the numbers in the cells must be all different in each column and each line, and that in each square we must find all the numbers from 1 to 9. Here constraints can be expressed using the specialized n-ary constraint AllDifferent [12]. Complex problems are usually naturally modeled with constraints involving a large number of variables. Historically, research in this area has focussed on binary constraints, i.e. constraints using only two distincts variables. Then some transformations allowing to translate a non-binary problem containing constraints involving more than two variables, into an equivalent binary problem have been proposed, one of them is the Hidden Variable Encoding (HVE) [13], well-known in the Constraint Programming community. In this paper, we formalize this encoding in Coq and prove that it does provide an equivalent encoding, in the sense that any solution of the encoding binary problem can be translated into

© Springer Nature Switzerland AG 2021
M. Hanus and C. Sacerdoti Coen (Eds.): WFLP 2020, LNCS 12560, pp. 117–128, 2021.
https://doi.org/10.1007/978-3-030-75333-7_7

a solution of the original non-binary problem and vice-versa. Furthermore if the original problem is unsatisfiable, then the encoding is also unsatisfiable and vice-versa.

This formal development related to HVE is used to extend the formally verified constraint binary solver developed in Coq by Carlier, Dubois and Gotlieb in 2012 [5], called CoqbinFD, making it a solver able to solve any problem. As far as we know, we provide here the first non-binary constraint solver (for finite domains) formally verified, extracted from a Coq development. It can serve as a reference solver for testing other constraint solvers. It can be compared to the verified LTL model checker developed in Isabelle/HOL proposed as a reference implementation in [8]. It is also a brick of a formal library dedicated to formalize results and classical algorithms about constraints, in the spirit of the project IsaFoL (Isabelle formalisation of Logic)[1] which includes e.g. the formalisation in Isabelle/HOL of a CDCL-based SAT solver using efficient imperative data structures [9].

In [6], we have presented such an encoding verified in Coq for ternary constraints only. This intermediate step was helpful to achieve the n-ary generalization. The two Coq formalisations are close and follow the same process. The main lemmas and theorems are if not identical, very close to each other. The reason why we have first done the ternary case is historical: the translation was implemented in OCaml to encode non-binary arithmetic constraints as a set of ternary constraints (it can always be done as long as only binary and unary operators occur in the non-binary constraint) in order to use CoqbinFD. Then we decided to push this transformation into Coq and to verify it for finally achieve the formalisation we present in this paper. The ternary version does not take into account extensional constraints whereas it is the case here.

The paper is organized as follows. Section 2 briefly presents the notion of constraint satisfaction problem, the main ingredients of a constraint solver and the Hidden Variable Encoding. Section 3 describes the Coq formalisation of the Hidden Variable Encoding and highlights the proven properties. Then Sect. 4 introduces the main characteristics of CoqbinFD. Section 5 presents the extended solver, obtained by reusing CoqbinFD and also some experimentations. We conclude in the last section.

2   Background

A *Constraint Satisfaction Problem* (csp for short) or network of constraints [10] is a triple (X, D, C) where X is a set of variables, C is a set of constraints over X and D is a function that associates a domain $D(x)$ to each variable x in X. In our context, we exclusively consider finite domains. Constraints are relationships between variables, each taking a value in their respective domain: constraints restrict possible values that variables can take. As often in CP literature, we assume that constraints are normalized, meaning that two distinct

---

[1] https://bitbucket.org/isafol/isafol/wiki/Home.

constraints cannot hold over exactly the same variables. The arity of a constraint is the number of its variables (assumed as distinct). A n-ary csp contains k-ary constraints with $k \leq n$. A csp is said non-binary as soon as it contains a constraint whose arity is strictly greater than 2. We do not consider unary constraints since the constraint can be directly taken into account in the domain. A solution is defined as a total assignment of the csp variables which satisfies all the constraints simultaneously.

Let us consider as an example the following non-binary csp (X, D, C) where $X = \{x_1, x_2, x_3, x_4, x_5, x_6\}$, $D(v) = \{0, 1\}$ for all v in X and $C = \{c_1 : x_1 + x_2 + x_6 = 1, c_2 : x_1 + x2 - x_3 + x_4 = 1, c_3 : x_4 + x_5 - x_6 \geq 1, c_4 : x_2 + x_5 - x_6 = 0, c_5 : x_1 \geq x_6\}$ inspired from [19]. It has a unique solution defined as $\{x_1 \mapsto 1, x_2 \mapsto 0, x_3 \mapsto 1, x_4 \mapsto 1, x_5 \mapsto 0, x_6 \mapsto 0\}$.

A constraint solver usually alternates propagation and exploration. Propagation prunes the domains of the variables, removing inconsistent values, using the constraints. This step can be decomposed in two interleaved routines: filtering that removes inconsistent values from the domains of the variables of one constraint and propagation that determines the constraints that have to be visited after a filtering step until a fixpoint is reached. Exploration enumerates values for some variables and may backtrack on these choices if necessary. The propagation step enforces a local consistency property that characterizes some necessary conditions on values to belong to solutions. There exist many different local consistencies, e.g. arc consistency, path consistency or bound consistency [3]. One of the oldest is arc consistency - AC for short - (when applied to binary constraints) or generalized arc consistency - GAC for short - (as a generalization of AC to n-ary constraints). Let c be a constraint of a csp (X, D, C) whose variables are $x_1, x_2 \dots x_k$. The constraint c is (generalized) arc consistent with respect to the csp if and only if for each variable x_i, for each value v in $D(x_i)$, there exist possible values for the other variables of the constraint c that make it true. Thus filtering c consists in removing the values of $x_1, x_2 \dots x_k$ that invalidate that property. In the previous example, c_1 is generalized arc consistent with respect to the given csp. However if we modify the domain of x_2 as the singleton $\{1\}$, c_1 is not anymore generalized arc consistent because when x_1 has the value 1, there is no value for x_2 that can make the constraint true. In such a case, a filtering algorithm would remove the value 1 from the domain of x_1.

Decomposition of non-binary constraints into equivalent binary constraints is a subject that has been widely discussed in the CP community and for quite a long time. A well-known transformation for constraint satisfaction problems with finite domains is the Hidden Variable Encoding (HVE) [13]. Recognized as having nice theoretical properties [11]. In HVE, every non-binary constraint is associated with a variable whose domain is the set of all possible tuples of the original constraint, i.e. the set of tuples (of values of involved variables in the constraint) that satisfy the constraint. Such a variable is called a *dual variable* and written v_c if c denotes the constraint. Thus the variables of the equivalent binary csp are the variables of the original csp called *original variables* and the dual variables. The domains of the original variables remain identical to their domain in the original csp. Original non-binary constraints do not appear anymore in the binary encoding; they are replaced by *hidden constraints* between a dual variable and each of the original variables in the constraint represented by the dual variable. A hidden constraint enforces the condition that a value of the original variable must be the same as the value assigned to it by the tuple that is the value of the dual variable [2]. In the following we denote them informally as projections: $proj_1, proj_2, \ldots$ A mathematical definition of this transformation (called the *hidden transformation*) can be found in [2] (see Definition 7).

As an illustration, the binary csp resulting from the HVE transformation applied on the example presented previously has 10 variables: the 6 original ones and 4 dual variables v_{c_1}, v_{c_2}, v_{c_3} and v_{c_4}. Domains of original variables remain identical whereas domains of the dual variables are such that

$$D(v_{c_1}) = \{(0,0,1),(0,1,0),(1,0,0)\},$$
$$D(v_{c_2}) = \{(0,0,0,1),(0,1,0,0),(0,1,1,1),(1,0,0,0),(1,0,1,1),(1,1,1,0)\},$$
$$D(v_{c_3}) = \{(0,1,0),(1,0,0),(1,1,0),(1,1,1)\} \text{ and}$$
$$D(v_{c_4}) = \{(0,0,0),(0,1,1),(1,0,1)\}.$$

There are 14 binary constraints: the original binary constraint c_5 and 13 hidden constraints, e.g. $proj_1(v_{c_2}, x_1)$, $proj_3(v_{c_4}, x_6)$.

3 Coq Formalisation of HVE Translation

3.1 N-ary Constraint Satisfaction Problem

The Coq formalisation follows the definition given previously, a csp is encoded as a record, of type *network_n* (see its definition in the code snippet below) containing a list of variables, a map from variables to domains (of type *domain_n*), represented as lists of values and a list of constraints. Types of variables (*variable_n*) and values (*value_n*) are abstract, they can be further defined either in Coq or in OCaml when extraction is used. We expect *value_n* and *variable_n* to be equipped with a strict total order and a decidable equality. Constraints (see below the definition of the type *constraint_n*), either binary or non-binary, are also abstract but the arity of a constraint is made explicit. It means that the type of basic constraints (*basic_constraint*) is abstract, equipped with a function to get the variables and an abstract interpretation function (as in CoqbinFD). A non-binary constraint is defined by a value of the abstract type *OP*, its arity and a list of variables. In order to be as general as possible, we consider extensional constraints as well as intentional ones. In the former case, the semantics is given as a list of acceptable tuples, in the latter case, a boolean function is expected. Constraint c_1 of the example given in Sect. 2 is represented as *Nary3 p1 [x1 ; x2 ; x6]* where *p1* is associated to the interpretation function $f(a,b,c) := a + b + c - 1 = 0$.

```
Inductive constraint_n : Set :=
| Bin : basic_constraint → constraint_n
| Nary : OP → nat → list variable_n → constraint_n.

Inductive interpretation : Set :=
```

| *Extension* : *list* (*list value_n*) → *interpretation*
| *Intention* : (*list value_n* → *bool*) → *interpretation*.

Record *network_n* : **Type** :=   *Make_cspn* {
   CVarsn : *list variable_n* ;
   Domsn : *domain_n*;
   Cstsn : *list constraint_n*
  }.

Our formalisation choice requires some extra properties about the input constraints language definition, in particular about the interpretation functions, for example *basic_interp* should only be defined for lists of length 2 (should fail for other cases) or the table defining an extensional k-ary constraint should only contain tuples with k components. These requirements can be checked at extraction time, e.g. by testing. They appear in our Coq development as axioms or parameters, in a weak form discovered during the proof of some properties.

Parameter *interp_op_length_extension* : ∀ *op ar table*,
interp_op op ar = *Extension table* → ∀ *l*, *In l table* → *length l* = *ar*.

The modeling of constraints is as simple as possible. It allows ill-formed constraints. The ability to deal with potentially ill-formed constraints makes the definition of some functions easier. We define well-formedness in a separate way as the predicate named *network_inv_n* which specifies the following requirements:

1. variables in constraints are exactly the ones that are listed in the csp and defined in the domain map;
2. constraints are normalized, meaning that they do not have the same set of variables;
3. any constraint has distinct variables;
4. in the case of a constraint of arity k represented by *Nary op k l*, the length of the list of variables l is exactly k, with k strictly greater than 2;
5. the tuples defining an extensional constraint must have components compatible with the domains of the related variables.

The property of well-formedness is implicitly introduced when needed.

An alternative way would have been to use dependent types for constraints, giving to the constructor *Nary* the following type *forall n, vector n* → *OP n* → *constraint_n* where *vector n* is the type of lists of length n and *OP n* the dependent version of the type *OP*. So a lot of types would become dependent. Another reason not to use dependent types is that we want to be able to easily define the constraints language in OCaml that does not provide such dependent types. A last reason is that the formalisation presented in this paper generalizes the proofs done for ternary constraints [6] and follows the same line.

3.2   Binary Constraint Satisfaction Problem

A binary csp (as it is encoded in CoqbinFD) has a very similar representation, it is a record containing a list of variables, a table that maps variables to finite domains and a list of binary constraints. We define in this subsection the variables, the values and the constraints of a binary csp resulting from the HVE translation. The type of variables, *variable*, is defined inductively and reflects that variables are either original variables (introduced by the constructor *OVar*) or hidden variables (constructor *HVar*). The latter variables are defined w.r.t an original constraint. We make explicit this association in the way we build variables. For example, the hidden variable v_{c_1} of the example given in Sect. 2 is encoded in Coq as *HVar p1 3 [x1; x2; x6]*.

Inductive *variable* :=
| *OVar* : *variable_n* → *variable*
| *HVar* : *OP* → *nat* → *list variable_n* → *variable*.

The type of values, *value*, is also defined inductively, it distinguishes raw values, which are the original variables values, from tuples which are the hidden variables values.

Inductive *value* :=
| *Raw_value* : *value_n* → *value*
| *Tuple* : *nat* → *tuple* → *value*.

A decidable equality and a strict order are defined for both types, following from the required equalities and orders on *value_n* and *variable_n*.

We can now define the type *constraint* whose values are the original binary constraints and the hidden constraints. In our example, the hidden constraint between v_{c_1} and the second original variable is represented in Coq by *Proj p1 3 [x1; x2; x6] 1 x2*. We prove the properties on the constraint language required by CoqbinFD, e.g. any constraint has distinct variables.

Inductive *constraint* : **Set** :=
| *Basic* : *basic_constraint* → *constraint*
| *Proj* : *OP* → *nat* → *list variable_n* → *nat* → *variable_n* → *constraint*.

3.3   HVE Transformation

The Coq function, *translate_csp_n*, that translates a non-binary csp into a binary csp, closely follows the presentation in Sect. 2 and the mathematical definition given in [2]. It uses several intermediate functions, in particular the function *expand* that computes the domain of a hidden variable, as a list of tuples, from the interpretation function and the domains of the ordinary variables of the constraint corresponding to the hidden variable. The computed domain contains only the tuples that satisfy the interpretation. In the case of an extensional non-binary constraint, the domain of the corresponding hidden variable is obtained by copying the table given as its interpretation. It also uses the function *cstsnTocsts2* which computes, for a list of constraints, the list of original binary and hidden constraints and the list of hidden variables coupled with their list of tuples computed with the help of *expand*. The ordinary binary constraints of the original csp and the corresponding domains are just copied modulo some elementary rewriting. The map containing the domains of the hidden variables is built with the help of the function *new_domain*.

Except some minor differences and the definition of the function *expand*, the function is similar to the one in the ternary case [6].

Definition *translate_csp_n cspn* :=
match (*cstsnTocsts2* (*Cstsn cspn*) (*Domsn cspn*)) **with**
| *None* ⇒ *None*
| *Some* (*cs*, *lvdv*) ⇒ *Some* (*Make_csp*
  (*List.app* (*List.map* (**fun** *x* ⇒ *OVar x*) (*CVarsn cspn*)) (*List.map* **fst** *lvdv*))
  (*new_domain* (*mapn_to_raw* (*Domsn cspn*) (*CVarsn cspn*)) *lvdv*)
  cs)
end.

Note that *translate_csp_n* may fail when *cstsnTocsts2* tries to access the domain of unknown variables. We prove that if the non-binary csp is well-formed then the translation does not fail:

Lemma *network_inv_n_translate_None_False* : ∀ *cspn*,
network_inv_n cspn → ¬ (*translate_csp_n cspn* = *None*).

We also prove that the binary csp obtained by HVE is well-formed if the original csp is well-formed:

Lemma *translate_cspn_network_inv* : ∀ *cspn csp*,
network_inv_n cspn → *translate_cspn cspn* = *Some csp* →
  network_inv csp.

3.4   Focus on Tuples and Extraction

Let us focus on the *expand* function that, in the case of an intentional constraint, computes the set of tuples. It is merely the computation of the cartesian product of k lists if the arity of the constraint is k. We first compute the result as a list of lists (of length k) representing the tuples. Then we turn these lists into tuples whose type is abstract with the help of an abstract function *tuple_from_list* introduced as a parameter. Yes, this step requires a computational overhead but it allows some flexibility at extraction time. For example we can map the type *tuple* to the OCaml *array* type in order to benefit from a constant time access. We can also keep lists by mapping *tuple_from_list* to the identity function.

Besides *tuple_from_list*, we need two other functions: *tuple_to_list* (of type *nat* → *tuple* → *list value_n*) and *proj_tuple* (of type *nat* → *tuple* → *value_n*). The first one is not used in the translation itself but only in the proofs. These functions are specified by three properties or axioms which are given below:

Parameter *tuple_to_from_list* : ∀ *a* ,
tuple_to_list (*length a*) (*tuple_from_list a*) = *a*.

Parameter *proj_tuple_nth_error* : ∀ *n n0 t v0*,
$n > 0$ → $n0 < n$ →
proj_tuple n0 t = *v0* ↔ *nth_error* (*tuple_to_list n t*) *n0* = *Some v0*.

Parameter *length_tuple_to_list* : $\forall$ *n t*,
length (tuple_to_list n t) = *n*.

In order to gain some more confidence when we extract OCaml code from the Coq code, we have tested these three properties using the QuickChick property testing tool for Coq programs [7] with 10 000 test cases randomly generated. It allowed the discovery of a missing hypothesis (the blue one in the second statement).

An alternative could be to use primitive persistent arrays in the Coq code for implementing tuples (without going through intermediate lists). The type of such arrays is axiomatized. Primitive arrays internally are implemented using a persistent data structure. This has been integrated into a very recent version of Coq while it was previously available as a separate implementation [1]. We plan to experiment with these primitive arrays. However cartesian product of domains implemented in the *expand* function is a bit more complicated when dealing with arrays.

A last proposition could be to implement tuples as finite functions, and then to use the coq library proposed by Sakaguchi in [16] to extract these tuples to OCaml arrays.

3.5   Correctness of the HVE Translation

To prove the correctness of the translation, we prove that satisfiability is preserved by the HVE translation. Two related properties are illustrated below.

A solution is defined as usual as an assignment of the csp variables which is total, valid (i.e. values are compatible with the domains) and locally consistent (i.e. making each constraint satisfied). It is implemented as a map from variables to values. A solution of a non-binary csp (resp. a binary encoding csp) is characterized by the predicate *solution_n* (resp. *solution*).

Lemma *translate_nosol* states that if the original non-binary csp is UNSAT (i.e. it admits no solution) then the binary encoding is also UNSAT. Lemma *translate_complete* explains that if the non-binary csp admits a solution, then its mapping to the hidden and original variables (computed by the function *translate_sol_n*) is a solution of the binary encoding.

Lemma *translate_nosol*: $\forall$ *cspn csp* ,
  network_inv_n cspn $\rightarrow$ *translate_csp_n cspn* = *Some csp* $\rightarrow$
  ($\forall$ *a*, $\neg$ *(solution a csp)*) $\rightarrow$ $\forall$ *an*, $\neg$ *(solution_n an cspn)*.

Lemma *translate_complete*: $\forall$ *an cspn csp*,
  network_inv_n cspn $\rightarrow$ *translate_csp_n cspn* = *Some csp* $\rightarrow$
  solution_n an cspn $\rightarrow$ *solution (translate_sol_n an cspn) csp*.

3.6   Local Consistencies

We have completed the formalisation by the proof of a result about local consistency: if the original csp is generalized arc consistent then its binary encoding is arc consistent. Unsurprisingly, the proof of this property reuses a large part of the script and intermediate lemmas developed for soundness and completeness. The interesting point worth noticing is that this proof requires the introduction of the requirement 5 in *network_inv_n* specifying the proper formation of tuples defining an extensional constraint.

4   Brief Presentation of the Formally Verified Solver CoqbinFD

In this section we briefly describe the binary solver CoqbinFD that we want to reuse. For more details please consult [5]. An important point in this development and crucial for the present work is its genericity. In the following we mainly emphasize the requirements about the generic parameters. The solver is indeed parameterized by the type of variables (*variable*) and values (*value*) and also by the constraint language (*constraint*). In Coq, these types are abstract, assumed to accept a decidable equality. It is also assumed that the semantics of the constraints is given by an interpretation function as a Boolean function of the values of its two variables and a function that retrieves, for any constraint, its two variables. So a constraint is abstracted as a relation over two distinct variables, represented by an interpretation predicate. These types and functions must be defined either in Coq or OCaml in order to use the extracted solver in a particular context. Here they are given Coq concrete values according to HVE.

A csp is defined as a record of type *network_csp* consisting of a finite list of variables (*CVars* field), a finite list of constraints (*Csts*) and a map (*Doms*) associating each domain with its variable, here a finite list of values. A predicate (*network_inv*) specifies the well-formedness of a csp: the entries of the domain map are exactly the variables of the csp, variables appearing in the constraints are exactly those declared, constraints are normalized and finally the two variables of any constraint are distinct.

The solving process is based on arc consistency, it implements a generic version of the propagation algorithm AC3 [10], allowing the use of AC2001 [10]. However here, it is transparent, the binary solver being used as a black-box.

5   Extension of the Solver CoqbinFD to Non-binary Constraints

We propose to build a constraint solver able to deal with binary and non-binary constraints by extending the CoqbinFD solver (whose main function is the *solve_csp* function) with the HVE translation acting as a pre-processor and the solution translation acting as a post-processing. The different steps are illustrated on Fig. 1.

The extended solver is mainly embodied by the following *solve_n* function which follows the steps of Fig. 1 and is built using the tactic Program [17] (as its counterpart in CoqbinFD):

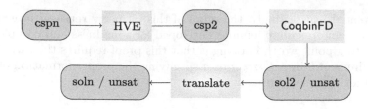

Fig. 1. Behavior of the non-binary solver

Program Definition *solve_n* (*cspn* : *network_n*) (*Hn*: *network_inv_n cspn*)
  : {*res* : *option* (*assign_n*) | *result_n_ok res csp*} :=
match (*translate_csp_n cspn*) with
  None ⇒ *None*
| *Some csp* ⇒ match (*solve_csp csp _*) with
        None ⇒ *None*
        | *Some a* ⇒ *Some* (*translate_sol a cspn.CVarsn*)
      end
end.

The type of the result is a kind of subtype *à la PVS*, it describes not only the type of the computed result *res* (*None* or a solution) but it also contains a proof that the result is sound (specified by the predicate *result_n_ok*), i.e. if the result is *None* then the original csp has no solution and if it is *Some a*, then *a* is a solution of the original csp. This definition generates proof obligations that correspond to the expected properties of the result. Another proof obligation comes from the underscore appearing in the call of *solve_csp* that expects as a third argument a proof that its second argument is well-formed. This proof obligation is solved by the lemma *translate_cspn_network_inv* shown previously in Subsect. 3.3.

Completeness of the extended solver is also proved. It follows from the completeness of CoqbinFD and from the properties of the *translate_sol_n* function regarding solutions.

The main task to extend CoqbinFD to n-ary constraints is to provide the binary encoding exactly as it is expected by CoqbinFD. As this solver is generic in the input constraint language, the task was made easier.

After extraction, we ran the extended solver (with the AC3 instance of CoqbinFD) to solve some problems. First we have used it with binary and ternary csps, for non-regression testing. The time overhead is not significant. We also solved some problems, intensional and extensional ones, from the XCSP2.1 library [15] where csps are represented as XML definitions. For example the problem named `normalized_g_4x4` with 16 variables with {0, 1} as domain and 15 constraints with arity from 3 to 5 is solved in 0.0033 sec on a laptop (2,3 GHz Intel Core i5 8 Go 2133 MHz LPDDR3) whereas for the problem known as `normalized-graceful-K2-P3` with 15 variables (whose domain is either 0..9 or 1..9) and 60 constraints, 9 of them being ternary and the rest being binary, we obtain a solution within 2.8 s.

The manual transcription of XCSP2.1 problems in OCaml is however tedious and error prone. Our solver could be completed with a tool allowing the translation of XML definitions into OCaml or Coq definitions. Following Stergiou and Samaras in [18], we could obtain a better efficiency by using specialized arc consistency and search algorithms for the binary encodings requiring to further prove some variants for propagation and exploration algorithms.

6 Conclusion

In this paper we have formalized in Coq the well-known Hidden Variable Encoding that performs the translation of a non-binary constraint satisfaction problem into an equivalent binary constraint satisfaction problem. This translation is used to extend the CoqbinFD solver, developed in Coq several years ago. The Coq code is available at www.ensiie.fr/~dubois/HVE_nary. From the whole Coq development, an OCaml executable solver can be extracted. It can be considered as a reference implementation and used to test other solvers, for example the FaCiLe OCaml constraint library [4].

References

1. Armand, M., Grégoire, B., Spiwack, A., Théry, L.: Extending Coq with imperative features and its application to SAT verification. In: Kaufmann, M., Paulson, L.C. (eds.) ITP 2010. LNCS, vol. 6172, pp. 83–98. Springer, Heidelberg (2010). https://doi.org/10.1007/978-3-642-14052-5_8
2. Bacchus, F., Chen, X., van Beek, P., Walsh, T.: Binary vs. non-binary constraints. Artif. Intell. **140**(1), 1–37 (2002)
3. Bessière, C.: Constraint propagation. In: Handbook of Constraint Programming, chap. 3. Elsevier (2006)
4. Brisset, P., Barnier, N.: FaCiLe : a functional constraint library. In: CICLOPS 2001, Colloquium on Implementation of Constraint and LOgic Programming Systems, Paphos, Cyprus (2001)
5. Carlier, M., Dubois, C., Gotlieb, A.: A certified constraint solver over finite domains. In: Giannakopoulou, D., Méry, D. (eds.) FM 2012. LNCS, vol. 7436, pp. 116–131. Springer, Heidelberg (2012). https://doi.org/10.1007/978-3-642-32759-9_12
6. Dubois, C.: Formally verified decomposition of non-binary constraints into equivalent binary constraints. In: Magaud, N., Dargaye, Z. (eds.) Journées Francophones des Langages Applicatifs 2019. Les Rousses, France (2019)
7. Dénès, M., Lampropoulos, L., Paraskevopoulou, Z., Pierce, B.C.: QuickChick: property-based testing for Coq (2014)
8. Esparza, J., Lammich, P., Neumann, R., Nipkow, T., Schimpf, A., Smaus, J.-G.: A fully verified executable LTL model checker. In: Sharygina, N., Veith, H. (eds.) CAV 2013. LNCS, vol. 8044, pp. 463–478. Springer, Heidelberg (2013). https://doi.org/10.1007/978-3-642-39799-8_31
9. Fleury, M., Blanchette, J.C., Lammich, P.: A verified SAT solver with watched literals using imperative HOL. In: Andronick, J., Felty, A.P. (eds.) 7th ACM SIGPLAN International Conference on Certified Programs and Proofs, CPP 2018, Los Angeles, CA, USA, pp. 158–171. ACM (2018)

10. Mackworth, A.: Consistency in networks of relations. Artif. Intell. **8**(1), 99–118 (1977)
11. Mamoulis, N., Stergiou, K.: Solving non-binary CSPs using the hidden variable encoding. In: Walsh, T. (ed.) CP 2001. LNCS, vol. 2239, pp. 168–182. Springer, Heidelberg (2001). https://doi.org/10.1007/3-540-45578-7_12
12. Régin, J.-C.: A filtering algorithm for constraints of difference in CSPs. In: 12th National Conference on Artificial Intelligence (AAAI 1994), pp. 362–367 (1994)
13. Rossi, F., Petrie, C.J., Dhar, V.: On the equivalence of constraint satisfaction problems. In: ECAI, pp. 550–556 (1990)
14. Rossi, F., van Beek, P., Walsh, T.: Handbook of Constraint Programming. Elsevier Science Inc., USA (2006)
15. Roussel, O., Lecoutre, C.: XML representation of Constraint networks: format XCSP 2.1. CoRR, abs/0902.2362 (2009)
16. Sakaguchi, K.: Program extraction for mutable arrays. Sci. Comput. Program. **191**, 102372 (2020)
17. Sozeau, M.: Subset coercions in Coq. In: Altenkirch, T., McBride, C. (eds.) TYPES 2006. LNCS, vol. 4502, pp. 237–252. Springer, Heidelberg (2007). https://doi.org/10.1007/978-3-540-74464-1_16
18. Stergiou, K., Samaras, N.: Binary encodings of non-binary constraint satisfaction problems: algorithms and experimental results. J. Artif. Intell. Res. **24**, 641–684 (2005)
19. Stergiou, K., Walsh, T.: Encodings of non-binary constraint satisfaction problems. In: Hendler, J., Subramanian, D. (eds.) Sixteenth National Conference on Artificial Intelligence and Eleventh Conference on Innovative Applications of Artificial Intelligence, Orlando, Florida, USA, pp. 163–168. AAAI Press/The MIT Press (1999)

Constraint-Logic Object-Oriented Programming with Free Arrays

Hendrik Winkelmann$^{(\boxtimes)}$ ⓘ, Jan C. Dageförde ⓘ, and Herbert Kuchen

ERCIS, Leonardo-Campus 3, 48149 Münster, Germany
{hendrik.winkelmann,dagefoerde,kuchen}@uni-muenster.de

Abstract. Constraint-logic object-oriented programming provides a useful symbiosis between object-oriented programming and constraint-logic search. The ability to use logic variables, constraints, non-deterministic search, and object-oriented programming in an integrated way facilitates the combination of search-related program parts and other business logic in object-oriented applications. With this work we add array-typed logic variables ("free arrays"), thus completing the set of types that logic variables can assume in constraint-logic object-oriented programming. Free arrays exhibit interesting properties, such as indeterminate lengths and non-deterministic accesses to array elements.

Keywords: Constraint-logic object-oriented programming · Free arrays · Non-deterministic element access · Reference types

1 Motivation

In constraint-logic object-oriented programming (CLOOP), one of the remaining missing puzzle pieces is the ability to use logic variables in lieu of arrays. As a novel paradigm, CLOOP describes programming languages that add constraint-logic features on top of an object-oriented syntax. Most importantly, CLOOP offers logic variables, constraints, and encapsulated non-deterministic search, seamlessly integrated with features from object-oriented programming. As a blueprint for CLOOP languages, the **Mu**enster **L**ogic-**I**mperative Programming Language (Muli) [2] is a Java-based language that has been successfully used in the generation of artificial neural networks [5], for search problems from the domain of logistics, and for classical search problems [4]. So far, logic variables in Muli can be used instead of variables of primitive types [4] or in place of objects [6]. Adding support for array-type logic variables is another step on the path to achieving the full potential of CLOOP. Potential opportunities are illustrated with the code snippet in Listing 1. This snippet declares a logic array a, i.e., an array with an indeterminate number of elements and none of the elements is bound to a specific value. Moreover, it uses logic variables as indexes for accessing array elements, resulting in non-deterministic accesses.

Prior to this work, Muli supported the use of arrays with fixed lengths and logic variables as elements. In contrast, free arrays are logic variables with an

© Springer Nature Switzerland AG 2021
M. Hanus and C. Sacerdoti Coen (Eds.): WFLP 2020, LNCS 12560, pp. 129–144, 2021.
https://doi.org/10.1007/978-3-030-75333-7_8

```
int i free;
int j free;
int[] a free;
if (a[i] > a[j]) a[i] = a[j] else ...;
```

Listing 1. Snippet in which an array as well as the indexes for access are not bound.

array type that are not bound to specific values, i.e., the entire array is treated symbolically. In a free array, the individual elements as well as the number of the elements are not known. This work presents the introduction of free arrays into CLOOP and Muli. The paper starts off by providing a short introduction to the Muli programming language in Sect. 2. Afterwards, it presents the contributions of this work:

- Section 3 introduces and defines the concept of free arrays in a CLOOP language.
- Section 4 discusses how to handle non-deterministic accesses to array elements when a free variable is used as the index.
- These ideas are accompanied by the description of a prototypical implementation of free arrays in the runtime environment of Muli, specifying the handling of symbolic array expressions as well as the modified behaviour of array-related bytecode instructions (see Sect. 5).

Section 6 presents related work, followed by a short summary in Sect. 7.

2   Constraint-Logic Object-Oriented Programming with Muli

Our proposal is based on the constraint-logic object-oriented programming language Muli, which facilitates the integrated development of (business) applications that combine deterministic program logic with non-deterministic search. Muli is based on Java 8 and adds features that enable constraint-logic search [4]. A key feature of Muli is the ability to declare logic variables. Since logic variables are not *bound* to a specific value, they are called *free variables*. A free variable is declared using the **free** keyword, as shown in the following example:

```
int size free.
```

Syntactically, declaring a free integer array is valid, too:

```
int[] numbers free,
```

however, the behaviour of free arrays was not defined yet, so such a declaration resulted in an exception at runtime. In this paper this issue is addressed by an implementation of free arrays.

```
Solution<Integer>[] evens = Muli.getAllSolutions(() -> {
  int number free;
  if (number > 5) {
      throw Muli.fail();
  } else if (number < 0) {
    throw Muli.fail();
  } else {
      return number*2; } }
```

Listing 2. Search region that imposes constraints on a free variable number and returns an expression as its solution.

Following its declaration, a variable can be used in place of other (regular) variables of a compatible type, for instance as part of a condition:

```
if (size > 5)
```

As `size` is not bound, the condition can be evaluated to **true** as well as to **false**, given appropriate circumstances. Upon evaluation of that condition, the executing runtime environment non-deterministically takes a decision and imposes an appropriate constraint that supports and maintains this choice (for example, `size > 5` in order to evaluate the **true**-branch). To that end, the runtime environment leverages a constraint solver for two purposes: First, the constraint solver is queried to check whether the constraint system of an application is consistent, thus avoiding the execution of branches whose constraint system cannot be solved. Second, the constraint solver is used to find specific values for free variables that respect the imposed constraints.

Eventually, the runtime environment considers all alternative decisions. The result is a (conceptual) search tree, in which the inner nodes correspond to the points at which decisions can be taken, with one subtree per decision alternative [7]. The eventual outcomes of the execution (in particular, returned values and thrown exceptions) are the leaves of the tree. A returned value or a thrown exception is a solution of non-deterministic search. In addition, Muli provides the facility to explicitly cut execution branches that are not of interest by invoking the `Muli.fail()` method.

The execution behaviour of Muli applications is, for the most part, deterministic and additionally provides *encapsulated search*. Application parts that are intended to perform non-deterministic search need to be declared explicitly in the form of methods or lambda expressions. These parts are called *search regions*. In order to start search, a search region is passed to an encapsulated search operator (e.g., `Muli.getAllSolutions()`) that causes the runtime to perform search while collecting all found solutions. After execution finishes, the collected solutions are returned to the invoking (deterministic) part of the application. Exemplarily, consider the search region presented in Listing 2. For a logic variable number it imposes constraints s.t. $0 \leq$ number ≤ 5 by cutting execution branches that do not satisfy this constraint. Otherwise, the symbolic expres-

```
ArrayList<Integer> list = new ArrayList<>();
for (int i = 0; i < (int)(Math.random()*1000); i++)
  list.add(i);
int[] arr = new int[list.size()];
```

Listing 3. The length of an array is not necessarily known at compile time. This example snippet determines the length at runtime instead.

sion number*2 is returned and collected by `Muli.getAllSolutions()`, i.e., the presented search region returns the numbers $\{0, 2, 4, 6, 8, 10\}$.

Muli applications are executed on the Münster Logic Virtual Machine (MLVM) [4]. The MLVM is a custom Java virtual machine with support for symbolic execution of Java/Muli bytecode and non-deterministic execution of search regions. The MLVM represents non-deterministic execution in a search tree, in which the inner nodes are `Choice` nodes (with one subtree per alternative decision that can be taken) and the leaf nodes are outcomes of search, i.e., solutions or failures [7]. Executing a bytecode instruction with non-deterministic behaviour results in the creation of a `Choice` node that is added to the search tree. For example, executing an `If_icmpeq` instruction (that corresponds to evaluating an equality expression as part of an **if** condition) results in the creation of a `Choice` node with two subtrees, one per alternative outcome, provided that the result of `If_icmpeq` can take either value according to the constraints that have already been imposed.

3   Arrays as Logic Variables

Muli relies on the symbolic execution of Java/Muli bytecode, i.e., symbolic expressions are generated during the evaluation of expressions that cannot (yet) be evaluated to a single constant value. Therefore, adding support for free arrays implies introducing symbolic arrays into the execution core of the MLVM.

The length of arrays in Java (and, therefore, in Muli) does not need to be known at compile time, as the legal code example in Listing 3 demonstrates: The number of elements that the array `arr` holds will become known at runtime. The length is arbitrary, provided that it can be represented by a positive (signed) **int** value [13].[1] As a consequence, a free array that is declared using

```
T[] arr free
```

comprises

- an unknown number of elements, so that `arr.length` is a free **int** variable n, where $0 \leq n \leq$ `Integer.MAX_VALUE`, and
- one free variable of type `T` per element `arr[i]` with $0 \leq i <$ `arr.length`

---

[1] At least in theory, as the `Newarray` bytecode instruction takes an **int** value for the length. In practice, the actual maximum number of elements may be lower as it depends on the available heap size on the executing machine.

Treating the length of a free array `arr` as a free variable provides the benefit that the length can be influenced by imposing constraints over `arr.length`, i.e., by referring to the length as part of **if** conditions. Moreover, for an array `T[] arr` **free** the type of the individual array elements `arr[i]` depends on what `T` is:

- If `T` is a primitive type, each element is a simple free variable of that type.
- If `T` is an array type, the definition becomes recursive as each element is, in turn, a free array.
- If `T` is a class or interface type, each element is a free object. Therefore, the actual type T' of each element is $T' \preceq T$, i.e., an element's type is either `T` or a type that extends or implements `T`. We do not go into specifics on free objects, as they are not of particular relevance here. The interested reader is directed to [6] on that matter.

Java requires regular arrays to be initialized either using an array creation expression of the form `T[] arr = ` **new** `T[n];`, resulting in an array `arr` with n elements of type `T` [10, § 15.10.1]; or an array initializer such as **int**`[] arr = {1, 2};`, resulting in an integer array that holds exactly the specified elements [10, § 10.6]. For free arrays, this opens up alternative ways of declaring (and initializing) a free array in Muli.

Simple free variable declaration. First, following the syntax that is used to declare any free variable, `T[] arr` **free** declares a free array whose length and elements are indeterminate.

Modified array creation expression. Second, `T[] arr = ` **new** `T[n]` **free**`;` is a modified array creation expression that allows to specify a fixed length for the array (unless n is free) while refraining from defining any of the array elements.

Modified array initializer. Third, a modification of the array initializer expression facilitates specifying the length as well as some array elements that shall be free; e.g., **int**`[] a = {1, ` **free**`, 0};` would define an array with a fixed length with two constant elements and a free one at `a[1]`. Trivially, regardless of the chosen initializer, array elements can be modified after the array has been initialized using explicit assignment. For example, `a[1] = 2;` can be used to replace an element (for example, a free variable) with a constant, and **int** `i` **free**`; a[1] = i;` replaces the element at index 1 with a free **int** variable.

These considerations facilitate the initialization and subsequent use of logic variables that represent arrays or array elements. All three alternatives are useful and should therefore be syntactically valid. For example, Listing 4 combines the initialization of a free string array via a simple free variable declaration, followed by imposing a constraint over the array's length (with `Muli.`**fail**`()` effectively cutting the branch of execution in which that constraint would not be satisfied).

```
String[] outputLines free;
if (outputLines.length > 5) {
    throw Muli.fail();
} else {
    // <...>
}
```

Listing 4. Limiting a free array's length to at most five elements by imposing an appropriate constraint.

4   Non-deterministic Access to Array Elements

Reconsider the example snippet from a search region that is given in Listing 1: Free arrays become particularly interesting when array elements are accessed without specifying the exact index, i.e., with the index as a free variable (e.g., arr[i] where **int** i **free**). In the comparison a[i] > a[j], the array a as well as the indexes for access are free variables. For a more complex example, consider the application depicted in Listing 5. It shows a simple sorting algorithm. The algorithm is not particularly efficient, but rather serves to show how free arrays can be used in a Muli application and demonstrates the use of other Muli features as well. The general idea of Listing 5 is to find a permutation of the elements of b that leads to a sorted array a. In line 3 of Listing 5, a free array of indexes is introduced. In lines 8–10, the unbound elements of this array are used as indexes of the arrays usedIdx and a. The algorithm searches for a permutation s.t. the final array is sorted. Consequently, if an index is used more than once, the array idx does not represent a permutation and the current branch of the search fails (line 8). Then, another branch is tried after backtracking. If the considered permutation does not lead to a sorted array, the current branch of the search also fails, thus resulting in backtracking (line 12). The efficiency of the algorithm ultimately depends on the constraint solver on which the Muli runtime system relies. Currently, Muli offers using either JaCoP [12], Z3 [15] or a custom SMT solver from the Münster Generator for Glass-box Test Cases (Muggl [8]). Moreover, the MLVM provides a flexible solver component that facilitates the addition of alternative constraint solvers to the MLVM [3].

Accessing an array with a free index is a non-deterministic operation, because more than one array element (or even a thrown runtime exception) could be the result of the access operation. Subsequently, we present approaches that can be used for handling such non-deterministic accesses to arrays. This list of approaches is probably non-exhaustive as there may be additional alternatives.

A first and simple approach would be to branch over all possible values for the index i in case that there is an access to a[i] where i **free**. Effectively, this is the equivalent of a labeling operation, successively considering every array element as the result of the access. Clearly, this would lead to a huge search space and it is hence not a reasonable option in most cases.

```
 1  public class SimpleSort {
 2      public static int[] sort(int[] b) {
 3          int[] idx free;
 4          boolean usedIdx[] free;
 5          int[] a free;
 6          if (a.length != b.length) throw Muli.fail();
 7          for (int i = 0; i < b.length; i++) {
 8              if (usedIdx[idx[i]]) throw Muli.fail();
 9              a[idx[i]] = b[i];
10              usedIdx[idx[i]] = true; }
11          for (int i = 0; i < b.length-1; i++) {
12              if (a[i] > a[i + 1]) throw Muli.fail(); }
13          return a; }
14      public static void main(String[] args) {
15          int[] b = {1, 42, 17, 56, 78, 5, 27, 39, 12, 8};
16          Solution<Object> result =
17              Muli.getOneSolution(() -> sort(b));
18      } }
```

Listing 5. Simple sorting algorithm that leverages free arrays.

A second approach could store constraints that involve accesses to array elements with unbound indexes symbolically. In the example from Listing 1, this implies storing the expression a[i] > a[j] as a constraint. This approach is complex to handle. In our example, it would require that, after every change in the remaining domains for i or j, we would have to check whether there are still possible values for i or j such that a[i] > a[j] can be satisfied. In the worst case that means that we have to check the constraint for all remaining pairs of values for i and j. As a consequence, this approach would be nearly as complex as the first one, the only difference being that the satisfiability check can stop as soon as values for i or j have been detected which satisfy the constraint.

A third approach could delay the check of constraints with symbolic array expressions until the involved indexes assume concrete, constant values. This would be similar to the delayed processing of negation in Prolog [1]. However, in contrast to Prolog, the ongoing computation would still continue. At the latest, the constraint needs to be checked when leaving the encapsulated search space, possibly after implicit labeling. Alternatively, the Muli application could explicitly demand checking delayed constraints, and the MLVM could throw an exception indicating that there are still delayed constraints when trying to leave an encapsulated search before a check. This approach is relatively easy to integrate into the MLVM. However, a major disadvantage of this approach is that time is wasted for exploring parts of the search space which could have been excluded if we had checked the constraint earlier (and found it to be unsatisfiable). Even worse, the corresponding computations could have caused external side-effects which should have never happened. This is a problem since external

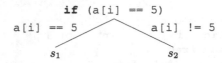

Fig. 1. Excerpt from a search tree, showing branch constraints that involve a symbolic expression for array element access, namely, a[i].

side-effects cannot be reverted on backtracking (e.g., file accesses or console output). Hence, they are discouraged in encapsulated search regions, especially in the case of delayed constraints. Moreover, there is no guarantee that checking the constraint at the end is easier than checking it immediately: If no additional constraints over i and j are encountered in the further evaluation, i and j may still assume the same values. Therefore, the delayed evaluation of the initial constraint is just as complicated as a strict evaluation.

A fourth and last approach could entirely forbid constraint expressions that involve unbound variables as array indexes. However, we feel that this approach is too restrictive. Moreover, it would not really provide new possibilities in Muli.

Unfortunately, all approaches that we could think of have some disadvantages. After comparing the advantages and disadvantages, we implemented the second approach in which constraints are evaluated eagerly for our prototype.

5   Implementation

Implementing the above considerations affects two areas of the runtime environment: First, the solver component must be capable of dealing with constraints over free arrays, i.e., it must be able to check a constraint system that comprises such constraints for consistency as well as to find values for the involved variables. Second, the execution core requires a modified execution semantics of array-related bytecode instructions. Subsequently, we outline our concept for an implementation in the MLVM.

5.1   Modelling Constraints over Free Arrays

Accessing an array element using a free variable as an index, e.g. a[i] with i **free**, yields a symbolic array expression (as described in Sect. 5.2). Using that as part of a condition, e.g., **if** (a[i] == 5) { s_1 } **else** { s_2 } causes the runtime environment to branch, thus creating a choice with two branches and appropriate constraints as illustrated in Fig. 1.

The way that a constraint involving symbolic array expressions (such as a[i] > a[j] from Listing 1) can be handled depends on the constraint solver. From the included constraint solvers, only Z3 provides native support for array theories (cf. [15,16]). Thus, the MLVM had to be extended in order to support such constraints. For handling constraints, the MLVM implements a *solver component* that abstracts from the actual underlying solver. This is achieved by offering a unified interface for the definition of symbolic expressions and constraints.

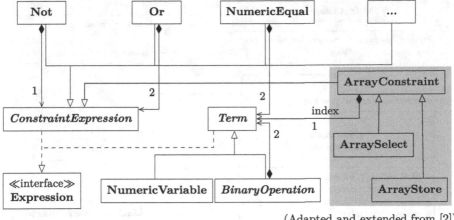

(Adapted and extended from [2])

Fig. 2. Augmenting the unified interface for the definition of constraints and expressions in order to add symbolic array expressions (additions shaded in red). (Color figure online)

Using a set of transformation methods, the defined constraints are transformed into a suitable representation for the respective solver that can then be queried from the MLVM using an adapter-pattern implementation. As a consequence, it is possible to add support for symbolic array expressions to the unified interface as illustrated in Fig. 2.

The required modifications to the Z3 solver component are illustrated in Fig. 3. In particular, we have added corresponding adapter classes.

The Context type is the main class provided by the official Z3 Java bindings [18]. In order to use it from the MLVM, the Z3SolverManager type manages the interaction of the Muli runtime with the Z3 solver by implementing the interface that is expected from an MLVM solver manager and delegating calls to an instance of Z3MugglAdapter. The Z3MugglAdapter transforms expressions and constraints specified in the unified interface to a corresponding representation for the Z3 Java bindings. For this, the Z3MugglAdapter configures and utilizes a Z3 context instance. First, the Z3 context is used to generate a solver. Thereafter, the Z3MugglAdapter transforms ConstraintExpressions into Z3 objects using the Z3 context instance. For instance, the Z3MugglAdapter would transform a symbolic array expression of the form a[i] == y (where a is a free integer array and l, i, v, y are free integers, with l being the free length of a) into the following (slightly simplified) commands for the Z3 solver[2]:

```
(declare-const a (Array Int Int))
(declare-const l)
(declare-const i Int)
```

---

[2] The semantics of the *select* and *store* array constraints (also see Fig. 2) are further explained in Section 5.3.

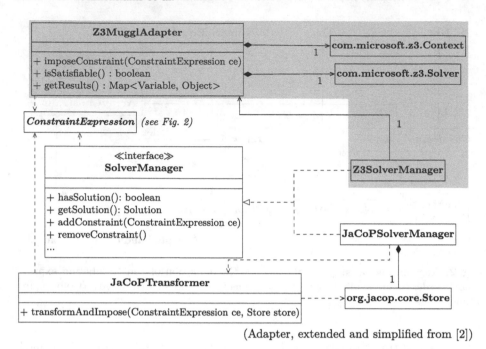

(Adapter, extended and simplified from [2])

Fig. 3. Modifications to the solver component of the MLVM in order to integrate the Z3 solver (additions shaded in pink).

```
(declare-const v Int)
(declare-const y Int)
(assert (< i 1))
(assert (>= i 0))
(assert (= v (select a i)))
(assert (= y v))
```

For each ConstraintExpression of Muli, the corresponding BoolExpr of Z3 is added to the Z3 solver's constraint stack. By calling push- and pop-methods of the solver object the Z3 solver can be used in an incremental fashion pushing backtracking points and popping them correspondingly [18].

The Z3 solver has been successfully used in the context of glass-box test case generation, e.g. with the Pex tool [17], even for applications that use symbolic arrays and indexes.

5.2   Conceptual Modifications to Bytecode Execution Semantics

The MLVM executes Java bytecode. Implementing the above considerations requires modifications to the execution semantics of the following bytecode instructions: Newarray, Arraylength, Xaload, Xastore (where X is replaced with a type, e.g., Iastore to store an array element of type **int**) [13].

`Newarray` is typically used in order to create an array on the heap. For the case of a free array, this requires the creation of an internal representation of the free array, comprising a `NumericVariable` for the `length` attribute (so that the length of a free array can become part of symbolic expressions) as well as a `Map<Term, T>` that will hold the individual elements. Storing the elements in an `ArrayList<T>` would account for the flexible size of free arrays, yet would conceptually fail for free indexes, since a concrete value for the index is not apparent. This representation will only be used internally by the MLVM. For Muli applications that use a free array its type is equivalent to that of a corresponding regular array.

The `Arraylength` bytecode instruction returns the length of an array [13, § 6.5]. If it is executed in the context of a free array, the instruction has to yield the symbolic representation of the free array's length. As an exception to that, if the logic variable for the length is already bound to a single value, `Arraylength` can return a constant.

The modifications to the `Xaload` and `Xastore` instructions work identically regardless of their type `X` and result in (potentially) non-deterministic execution. The `Xaload` instruction is the bytecode equivalent of accessing a single array element, e.g., `a[i]`, whereas `Xastore` is the equivalent of assigning a value to an array element, e.g., `a[i] = x`. Execution requires to make a distinction based on what is known about the length n of the involved free array (e.g., from constraints that have already been imposed on n). For `a[i]`, if `i` is definitely within the range $(0..n - 1)$, the behaviour is deterministic and results in a `ArraySelect` or `ArrayStore` constraint accordingly. Similarly, if `i` is outside of that range, the execution (deterministically) results in throwing a runtime exception of the type `ArrayIndexOutOfBoundsException`. In all other cases, the execution results in the creation of a non-deterministic choice, distinguishing successful access (yielding a symbolic expression) and the error case (yielding an exception) as alternative outcomes. Each alternative results in imposing appropriate constraints over `i` and n. Using backtracking, the MLVM will evaluate both alternatives successively.

5.3 Prototypical Implementation of Bytecode Execution Semantics

We have implemented a prototype which enables the execution of Muli programs with free arrays using the Z3 solver [15,16]. The implementation of free arrays extends the `Arrayref` class used by Muli to represent arrays. The resulting `FreeArrayref` class is used by the adjusted bytecode to distinguish between deterministic array behavior (`Arrayref`) and non-deterministic array behavior (`FreeArrayref`), i.e., allowing a variable sized array which accounts for free indexes. When declaring a free array, such as **int**[] idx **free**, a `FreeArrayref` is automatically generated, carrying a `Map<Term, Object>` for the elements in the array and a `NumericVariable` to represent its length. `Terms` here represent either an `IntConstant` for a concrete given value, or a `NumericVariable` for free variables.

The bytecode instruction `Arraylength` returns the length of the `FreeArrayref` as a possibly unbounded integer variable. In contrast, for usual `Arrayrefs` an integer constant is returned. More interestingly, the bytecode of `Xaload` and `Xastore` instructions has been adjusted to work with free arrays.

The procedure for all `Xaload` instructions has been implemented uniformly and is divided into two steps. In a first step two constraints are composed and evaluated. The first constraint represents a valid index access, i.e., the index must be larger or equal to zero and smaller than the length of the array. Furthermore, a *select* constraint (`= v (select a i)`) (see Sect. 5.1) is created. For this, first, if the current index is not present in the current free array a new free variable is generated at the index position of the array. If, for example, the free array contains integer values, a new free integer variable is generated. The result is stored in the `Map<Term, Object>` map using the `Term`, either an `IntConstant` or a `NumericVariable`, which is given as the index. On the other hand, if the index already resides within the free array, the value for it is used in the following. These values, i.e., the array, the index, and the value are then represented by objects of the Z3 solver: The free array is mapped to an array value a, the index to a value i, and the loaded value to a value v. In the further course of the program, each of the program's variables is represented by a Z3 counterpart, i.e., new select constraints will also target the same Z3 objects a, i, and v. The select constraint enforces that at index i, where i is not necessarily bound to a value yet, value v is positioned. This select constraint is then conjoined with the aforementioned index constraint.

The second constraint created in `Xaload` instructions represents constraints for an invalid index access, i.e., an access which would raise an `ArrayIndexOutOf-BoundsException`. For this, the index is either larger or equal to the length of the free array or the index is less than zero. The satisfiability of both constraints is evaluated. The result of these satisfiability checks is a potential branching point for the program: If either check holds, a choice point of one or two choices is generated. The implementation of the `Xaload` instructions will then proceed with its second step: Each of the feasible branches receives a corresponding marker. The marker indicates which of the cases is to be executed, i.e., whether an exception is to be thrown or if the usual semantics of the `Xaload` instruction [13] should be executed with the constraints given for the respective branch.

`Xastore` behaves similarly and its execution is also divided into the two corresponding steps. Aside from its semantics, `Xastore` instructions differ from `Xaload` instructions in that the former do not push a select constraint for valid index accesses. Rather, they enforce a *store* constraint: Expressions similar to (`= (store a1 i v) a2`) are pushed to the constraint solver. This constraint states that a value v is inserted into an array a1 at index i. In this context, a1 is immutable. Hence the output is a new array a2 which differs from a1 in the inserted value. As a consequence, we utilize a2 as the new representation for the respective free array. For this branch of execution, future constraints are connected with a2. If the `Xastore` instruction is backtracked, we again utilize al as the representation of the free array. By doing so, we enable the treatment of mutable arrays using the Z3 solver.

Checking constraints is currently done eagerly, i.e., our prototype implements the second approach mentioned in Sect. 4. Lastly, we enabled to skip the creation of ArrayIndexOutOfBoundsExceptions to allow for more concise formulations. Take, for example, Listing 5: The domain of values from the array idx is not limited. In consequence, each access usedIdx[idx[i]] potentially is illegal and we would have to restrict the domain of each value stored in idx. By setting a corresponding flag, the program will only regard valid index accesses.

5.4   Demonstration of Prototypical Implementation

We validated our implementation by means of several JUnit tests among which there is the SimpleSort example from Listing 5. SimpleSort will be discussed in the following. It is deemed a sound proof-of-concept example since it utilizes a manifold of features of free arrays while being intuitive to understand. These used features are comprised of indirect free index accesses using an index array, store and select constraints with free indexes (all within lines 8–10), as well as select constraints with concrete indexes (line 12). However, the example obviously is rather an illustrative choice than a competitive sorting algorithm, since it simply tries out multiple permutations of the input array. As such, the computation time is expected to vastly increase with the input list's size. We executed the SimpleSort::sort algorithm with a list size of 10, 20, 40, and 80 elements, disregarding potential ArrayIndexOutOfBoundsExceptions, using an AMD Ryzen 5 4500u CPU running Ubuntu 20.10. Each scenario has been executed five consecutive times. The examples as well as the test suite and code for free arrays in Muli are available under the GPL-3.0 license[3] (Table 1).

Table 1. Run times and standard deviations of executing SimpleSort with a varying number of elements.

Scenario	Mean run time (s)	Standard deviation of run time (s)
SimpleSort10	2.36	0.02
SimpleSort20	3.41	0.04
SimpleSort40	16.13	0.16
SimpleSort80	283.11	7.43

All in all, the run time behaves as expected. The execution time increases exponentially with the input size. That excludes the step from the SimpleSort10 to the SimpleSort20 scenario and might be explained by additional startup overhead including warming up the Java virtual machine. Still, the results produce a valid output.

---

[3] https://github.com/wwu-pi/muli/tree/free-arrays.

5.5   Limitations of Prototypical Implementation

Currently, the prototype does not support free arrays of free objects. The reason for this is the inherent complexity and mutability of free objects [6]. Free objects do not always have a deterministic type. Hence, their attributes and attribute types might differ between possible concrete classes. Still, they would have to be represented as the content of an array within Z3. Furthermore, similar to mutable arrays which we did address in this paper, mutable objects might prove difficult to represent in Z3: Each free object which is stored in a free array would have to be represented as a tuple of values. If an object which resides in a free array is to be altered, said representing tuple in Z3 must be altered as well while taking backtracking into account. In the future, we want to design an efficient approach to counteract this issue.

We also plan to implement the third approach of considering array constraints, as discussed in Sect. 4. As a consequence, the Muli runtime is going to allow developers to configure the system in order to choose an approach that best suits their respective search problem. The idea here is to accumulate select and store constraints and only push them to the constraint solver once a concrete solution is requested. Similar to this, comparisons of other approaches, e.g., an own logical layer which enables JaCoP to deal with array constraints, are left for future work. A quantitative evaluation will be able to show whether one approach is generally favourable over the other.

6   Related Work

A first approach to a symbolic treatment of arrays dates back to McCarthy's *basic theory of arrays* developed in 1962 [14]. It consists of just two axioms, one telling that if a value v is assigned to a[i] then a[i] later on has this value v. The other axiom essentially says that changing a[i] does not affect any other array element. These axioms are clearly not enough for handling free arrays in Muli. McCarthy's approach was extended to the *combinatorial array logic* by de Moura and Bjørner [16]. It is expressed by a couple of inference rules, which work on a more abstract level and do not address the processing of the search space. Nevertheless, these rules are among the theoretical foundations of Microsoft's Z3 SMT solver [15]. Based on this solver, support for arrays was included into Microsoft's test-case generator Pex [17] and into the symbolic code execution mechanism of NASA's Java Pathfinder, a model checker and test-case generator for Java programs [9]. In order to achieve the latter, Fromherz et al. mainly changed the semantics and treatment of the Xaload and Xastore bytecode instructions of their symbolic variant of the Java virtual machine. Their changes to these instructions are similar to our modifications of the MLVM, with the exception that the MLVM has a more sophisticated mechanism for backtracking and resuming an encapsulated search. The authors do not discuss approaches for dealing with the potentially huge search space caused by array constraints.

Also in the context of test-data generation, Korel [11] presented an array-handling approach which avoids the difficulties of free arrays and symbolic array indexes by resorting to a non-symbolic execution. Korel used a concrete evaluation in combination with dataflow analysis and so-called function minimization in order to reduce the search space. This approach is not suitable for a CLOOP language.

All the mentioned approaches stem from the domains of test-case generation and model checking. To the best of our knowledge, there is no other programming language that offers free arrays with symbolic array indexes.

7   Conclusion and Outlook

As a research-in-progress paper, this work presents approaches for the addition of free arrays to constraint-logic object-oriented programming, thus starting a discussion. The present paper discusses the characteristics and implementation aspects of free arrays. In particular, we address the symbolic treatment of the array length and symbolic array indexes based on constraints. Moreover, we propose a syntax for the declaration and initialization of free arrays. In addition, we discuss ways of dealing with non-deterministic accesses to array elements, proposing possible solutions to that end. The proposed concepts facilitate the use of logic arrays in the context of encapsulated, non-deterministic search that is interleaved with deterministic computations. Muli allows using arbitrary search strategies in order to use symbolic computations that involve arrays.

The foundations for further comparisons and research has been laid by an implementation and demonstration of free arrays for the Muli programming language. To achieve this implementation, the Z3 solver has been added to the MLVM as an alternative backend of the solver components so that symbolic array expressions can be leveraged. This allows for an exhaustive evaluation of the approaches in combination with different solvers in the future.

References

1. Apt, K., Bol, R.: Logic programming and negation: a survey. J. Log. Program. **19**(20), 9–71 (1994). https://doi.org/10.1016/0743-1066(94)90024-8
2. Dageförde, J.C.: An integrated constraint-logic and object-oriented programming language: the Münster logic-imperative language. Dissertation, University of Münster (2020)
3. Dageförde, J.C., Kuchen, H.: A constraint-logic object-oriented language. In: Proceedings of the 33rd ACM/SIGAPP Symposium on Applied Computing, pp. 1185–1194. ACM (2018). https://doi.org/10.1145/3167132.3167260
4. Dageförde, J.C., Kuchen, H.: A compiler and virtual machine for constraint-logic object-oriented programming with Muli. J. Comput. Lang. **53**, 63–78 (2019). https://doi.org/10.1016/j.cola.2019.05.001
5. Dageförde, J.C., Kuchen, H.: Applications of muli: solving practical problems with constraint-logic object-oriented programming. In: Lopez-Garcia, P., Giacobazzi, R., Gallagher, J. (eds.) Analysis, Verification and Transformation for Declarative Programming and Intelligent Systems. LNCS. Springer (2020)

6. Dageförde, J.C., Kuchen, H.: Free objects in constraint-logic object-oriented programming. In: Becker, J., et al. (eds.) Working Papers, European Research Center for Information Systems, vol. 32, Münster (2020)
7. Dageförde, J.C., Teegen, F.: Structured traversal of search trees in constraint-logic object-oriented programming. In: Hofstedt, P., Abreu, S., John, U., Kuchen, H., Seipel, D. (eds.) INAP/WLP/WFLP -2019. LNCS (LNAI), vol. 12057, pp. 199–214. Springer, Cham (2020). https://doi.org/10.1007/978-3-030-46714-2_13
8. Ernsting, M., Majchrzak, T.A., Kuchen, H.: Dynamic solution of linear constraints for test case generation. In: 2012 Sixth International Symposium on Theoretical Aspects of Software Engineering, pp. 271–274 (2012). https://doi.org/10.1109/TASE.2012.39
9. Fromherz, A., Luckow, K.S., Păsăreanu, C.S.: Symbolic arrays in symbolic PathFinder. ACM SIGSOFT Softw. Eng. Notes 41(6), 1–5 (2017). https://doi.org/10.1145/3011286.3011296
10. Gosling, J., Joy, B., Steele, G., Bracha, G., Buckley, A.: The Java® Language Specification - Java SE 8 Edition (2015). https://docs.oracle.com/javase/specs/jls/se8/jls8.pdf
11. Korel, B.: Automated software test data generation. IEEE Trans. Softw. Eng. 16(8), 870–879 (1990). https://doi.org/10.1109/32.57624
12. Kuchcinski, K.: Constraints-driven scheduling and resource assignment. ACM Trans. Des. Autom. Electron. Syst. 8(3), 355–383 (2003). https://doi.org/10.1145/785411.785416
13. Lindholm, T., Yellin, F., Bracha, G., Buckley, A.: The Java® Virtual Machine Specification - Java SE 8 Edition (2015). https://docs.oracle.com/javase/specs/jvms/se8/jvms8.pdf
14. McCarthy, J.: Towards a mathematical science of computation. In: Information Processing, Proceedings of the 2nd IFIP Congress 1962, Munich, Germany, North-Holland, 27 August–1 September 1962, pp. 21–28 (1962)
15. de Moura, L., Bjørner, N.: Z3: an efficient SMT solver. In: Ramakrishnan, C.R., Rehof, J. (eds.) TACAS 2008. LNCS, vol. 4963, pp. 337–340. Springer, Heidelberg (2008). https://doi.org/10.1007/978-3-540-78800-3_24
16. de Moura, L.M., Bjørner, N.: Generalized, efficient array decision procedures. In: Proceedings of 9th International Conference on Formal Methods in Computer-Aided Design, FMCAD 2009, 15–18 November 2009, Austin, Texas, USA, pp. 45–52. IEEE (2009). https://doi.org/10.1109/FMCAD.2009.5351142
17. Tillmann, N., de Halleux, J.: White-box testing of behavioral web service contracts with Pex. In: Bultan, T., Xie, T. (eds.) Proceedings of the 2008 Workshop on Testing, Analysis, and Verification of Web Services and Applications, Held in Conjunction with the ACM SIGSOFT International Symposium on Software Testing and Analysis (ISSTA 2008), TAV-WEB 2008, Seattle, Washington, USA, 21 July 2008, pp. 47–48. ACM (2008). https://doi.org/10.1145/1390832.1390840
18. Z3: Z3 Java Bindings API: Context (2019). https://z3prover.github.io/api/html/classcom_1_1microsoft_1_1z3_1_1_context.html

Author Index

Printed in the United States
by Baker & Taylor Publisher Services